PHYSICS MATTERS!

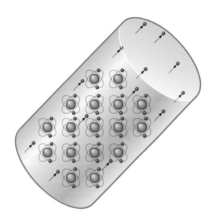

VOLUME 7
ELECTRIC CURRENT

Christopher Cooper

GROLIER
EDUCATIONAL

About this set

PHYSICS MATTERS! explains and illustrates the science of physics and its everyday applications. Physics is concerned with matter—the stuff from which everything is made—and with energy in all its various forms. To deal with such a wide-ranging subject in a logical way, the ten volumes in this set are organized as follows:
Volume 1—Matter; Volume 2—Mechanics; Volume 3—Heat; Volume 4—Light; Volume 5—Sound; Volume 6—Electric Charges; Volume 7—Electric Current; Volume 8—Magnetism; Volume 9—Electronics; Volume 10—Nuclear Physics
The topics within each volume are presented as self-contained modules, so that your understanding of the subject grows in linked stages. Each module is illustrated with color photographs, and there are diagrams that explain physical principles and the workings of scientific apparatus and machines that make use of them.

Pages at the end of each book give step-by-step details for activities (projects and experiments) that you can do for yourself. Each helps explain one of the main scientific principles dealt with in that particular volume. There is also a glossary that gives the meanings of scientific terms used, a list of other sources of reference (books and websites), followed by an index to all the volumes in the set. There are cross-references within volumes and from volume to volume to link topics for a fuller understanding.

Concept and planning: John O. E. Clark

Scientific authentication: Mick Nott and Graham Peacock

Published 2001 by Grolier Educational, Danbury, CT 06816

This edition published exclusively for the schools and library market

Planned and produced by Andromeda Oxford Limited
11-13 The Vineyard,
Abingdon, Oxon OX14 3PX, UK

Copyright © Andromeda Oxford Limited 2001

Project Director: *Graham Bateman*
Editors: *John Woodruff, Shaun Barrington*
Editorial Assistant: *Marian Dreier*
Picture Manager: *Claire Turner*
Production: *Clive Sparling*

Design & origination by Gecko

Printed in Hong Kong

Library of Congress Cataloging-in-Publication Data

Physics matters!
    p. cm.
Includes bibliographical references and index.
Contents: v.1.Matter—v.2.Mechanics—v.3.Heat—v.4.Light—v.5.Sound—v.6.
Electric charges—v.7.Electric current—v.8.Magnetism—v.9.Electronics—v.10.
Nuclear physics.
ISBN 0-7172-5509-3 (set: alk. paper)—ISBN 0-7172-5510-7 (v.1: alk. paper)—
ISBN 0-7172-5511-5 (v.2: alk. paper)—ISBN 0-7172-5512-3 (v.3: alk. paper)—
ISBN 0-7172-5513-1 (v.4: alk. paper)—ISBN 0-7172-5514-X (v.5: alk. paper)—
ISBN 0-7172-5515-8 (v.6: alk. paper)—ISBN 0-7172-5516-6 (v.7: alk. paper)—
ISBN 0-7172-5517-4 (v.8: alk. paper)—ISBN 0-7172-5518-2 (v.9: alk. paper)—
ISBN 0-7172-5519-0 (v.10: alk. paper)
    1. Physics—Juvenile literature. [1.Physics.] I. Grolier Educational (Firm)

QC25 P49 2001
530–dc21

                                        00-055160

Set ISBN 0-7172-5509-3
Volume 7 ISBN 0-7172-5516-6

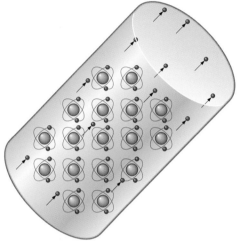

CONTENTS

HOW TO USE THIS SET

Each volume in this set deals with a particular subject in physics. Within each volume there is a series of modular entries, from two to six pages in length. The modules are ordered so as to present information in a logical way.

All modules start with a **main entry heading** that tells you the topic of that module—"Atomic structure", for example, or "Strain on solids". A short **summary** then introduces the main text. Each volume contains **boxed features** separate from the main text, which are short biographies of some of the most important physicists.

There are two types of illustrations, each with full **captions** to explain relevance. **Color photographs** depict examples and applications of the scientific principles being described. **Diagrams** are used to explain physical principles and add to the account being given in the main text. The diagrams have their own boxes and captions. Many diagrams are labeled to help you understand what is going on.

At the end, each volume contains up to nine scientific **projects** that show the basic principles of physics. The projects are designed to use everyday materials that are easily to hand—no special apparatus is required.

Main entry heading to a two-, four-, or six-page module

Summary introduces the topic

Diagrams help explain scientific principles

Running head indicates volume title

Captions explain the relevance of photographs or diagrams

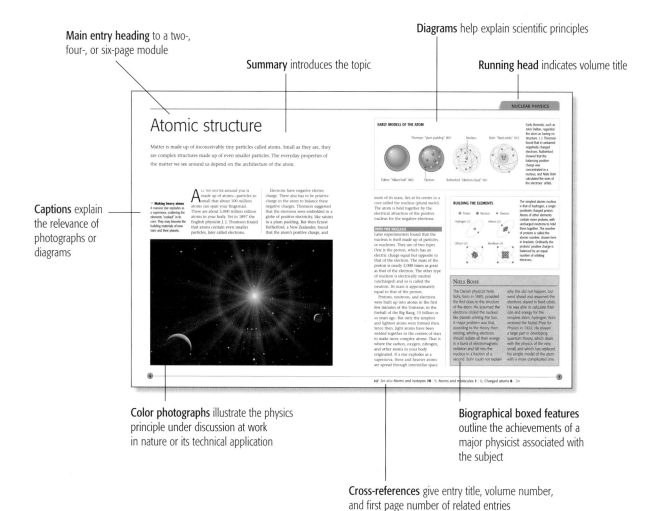

Color photographs illustrate the physics principle under discussion at work in nature or its technical application

Biographical boxed features outline the achievements of a major physicist associated with the subject

Cross-references give entry title, volume number, and first page number of related entries

A number of other features help you broaden your learning. At the beginning of each module, at the bottom of the right-hand page there are **cross-references** to related entries. They are given in the form of entry title, volume number, and page. Physics has its own special scientific terms, which are defined when they are first mentioned. In addition, each volume contains a two-page **glossary** to remind you of the meanings of any such unfamiliar terms. Every volume contains an **index** to the whole set, and there is a list of other books to read and websites to visit under the heading **further reading**.

INTRODUCTION TO VOLUME 7

Electric current consists of a flow of electrons through a conductor. Some materials conduct electricity better than others. Some—called insulators—do not conduct current at all. This volume looks at the conducting properties of various materials and goes on to describe ways of producing electric currents, both AC and DC. The second half of the book describes how electricity is used in the home, in industry, and in the world of communications.

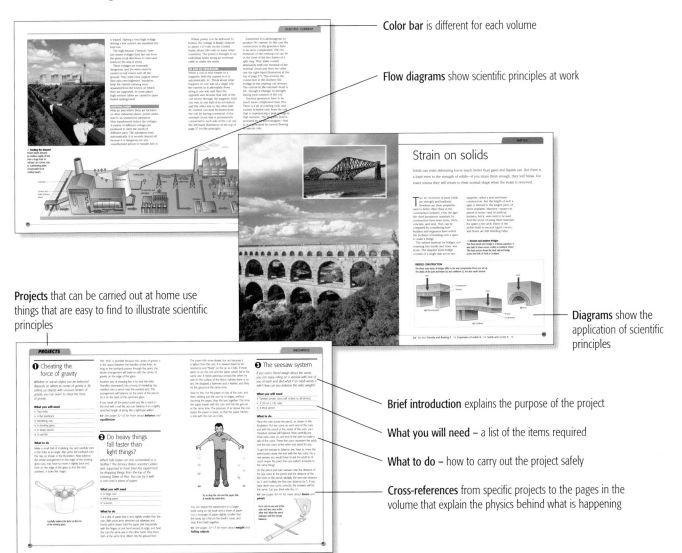

Color bar is different for each volume

Flow diagrams show scientific principles at work

Diagrams show the application of scientific principles

Projects that can be carried out at home use things that are easy to find to illustrate scientific principles

Brief introduction explains the purpose of the project

What you will need – a list of the items required

What to do – how to carry out the project safely

Cross-references from specific projects to the pages in the volume that explain the physics behind what is happening

Moving charges

An electric current consists of electrically charged particles in motion. Such currents produce effects that are useful to us in all kinds of ways, making electricity the workhorse of modern civilization. Electric currents can, for example, create heat, exert magnetic forces, and carry messages.

A LL MATTER IS made up of electrically charged particles. Every atom has a central core, or nucleus, that contains most of its mass and is positively charged. And whirling around it are much lighter, negatively charged particles that are called electrons.

∇ **High-wire act**
Linemen work on a high-voltage cross-country power line. We use the current in our own homes at a much lower voltage.

The forces between electrically charged particles are very strong. These powerful forces hold the atom together. But when equal amounts of positive and negative charge are close to each other, the effects of the charges cancel each other out, and a short distance away it is as if no charge at all were present. In normal atoms the positive charge on the nucleus is exactly balanced by the negative charge of the electrons. Electrical effects become noticeable when electrons are removed from atoms, leaving ions that have an unbalanced positive charge. (An ion is an atom or group of atoms with one or more electrons added or removed.)

When you comb your hair with a plastic comb, you sometimes see strands of hair attracted to the comb. This happens when electrons have been transferred from the comb to the hair, leaving positively charged atoms behind. The negative charges on the hair and the positive charges on the comb attract each other. This is an example of what is called static electricity.

Electric charge also shows its presence when it moves along a conductor as an electric current. When you switch on a light or a television set, electrons flow along the wires connecting the appliance to the electricity outlet in the wall and in the wires and cables connecting the outlet to the power plant. When you switch on a pocket calculator, very weak electric currents flow in the metal connections and the microchips inside the calculator.

Electric currents are important because they have so many different effects that we can use. They heat up the wires through which they flow, so they can be used in electric heaters, electric irons, and electric lamps. The currents also have magnetic effects. For example, rapidly varying electric current in a loudspeaker pulls on magnets in the loudspeaker's moving parts, which oscillate rapidly to produce sounds. Electric currents can also be used for signaling. Currents carry signals that represent sound to and from your telephone, they carry data in your computer, and they carry the information from which pictures are built up in your TV set. Electric currents made the information revolution possible.

Small current flowing in wire

Atom of
high-resistance
metal

Current flowing in wire

Electrons move

No current flowing in wire

Free electron

Atom of low-resistance metal

△ **Electrons on the move**
Metals are good conductors because electrons can easily become detached from their atoms and form a "sea" of electrons throughout the metal wire (bottom left). When a voltage is applied along the wire (middle section) the electrons drift along together in the same direction as an electric current. If the same voltage is applied to a wire of different metal, a different current flows. If the current is smaller—that is, if fewer electrons move—the metal is described as having a higher resistance than the first one (top right). Heat is generated whenever a current flows through a conductor. The heat generated depends on the resistance of the conductor and on the amount of current flowing through it—the higher the resistance, the greater is the amount of heat.

☞ See also Attraction and repulsion **6** : 8; Current and stored charge **7** : 12; Producing charge **6** : 6

Potential difference

Electric charges need a push to make them move. This push is called potential difference and is measured in volts. Power plants and batteries both create potential difference, on very different scales, in order to get electric currents flowing.

THE PHYSICAL FORCES you exert in combing your hair can move small amounts of charge. Pulling off an artificial-fiber shirt can have the same effect: you feel a tiny shock, and if you are in the dark, you can sometimes see sparks. When you walk on certain types of carpet, charge builds up on your body. You notice this happening when you touch a metal object, such as a faucet, and feel a small shock as the charge flows into it.

Charge flows easily through some materials, such as metals. They are called electrical conductors. It can hardly flow at all through others, such as rubber and most plastics. They are called electrical insulators. The cord to, say, a desk lamp is made of copper wires (along which the current flows) coated with plastic (through which the current cannot flow).

You will not get a shock, or see sparks, if you comb your hair with a metal comb. Electrons dislodged from your hair flow away through the metal immediately and cannot build up into a sizeable quantity of charge, as they can on a plastic comb.

MAKING CURRENTS FLOW

An electric battery is a way of making currents flow. When the two terminals are connected through conducting wires to a device such as a flashlight bulb, an electric current is driven through the device. In chemical reactions that take place inside the battery, electrons are separated from their atoms. The electrons are forced through the wires and then through the device. When the device is disconnected the electrons cannot move, and that brings the chemical reactions to a stop—just as blocking a highway can bring traffic to a halt a long way back.

Power plants use more powerful devices for making electric currents flow. Steam, generated using the heat of burning coal, oil, or gas, or from nuclear energy, is used to drive huge turbines. Electric generators coupled to the turbines produce high-voltage current that is distributed along cables that run across country.

In a wire in which current is flowing there are trillions of electrons in motion. But the electric charge is zero overall. The negative charge of the electrons is canceled out by the positive charge on the atoms that have lost their electrons.

If the circuit is broken, electrons immediately stop flowing. If they momentarily began to accumulate at the break or any other point in the circuit, their electric charge would repel others following behind, and

◁ **Electric locomotive**
Current flows from the high-voltage overhead lines and through the pantograph—the pickup gear on the top of the train. It travels through the locomotive's electric motors, turning shafts that drive the wheels.

☞ *See also* Current and stored charge **7** : 12; Direct and alternating **7** : 20; Electric fields **6** : 16

△ Portable power
In a newly excavated mine tunnel no power lines have yet been laid. Batteries provide the power for helmet lamps and other equipment.

instantly disperse the accumulation of charge. This is why electric current cannot flow unless there is an unbroken loop, called a circuit, that it can follow.

The "push" that drives electrons around a circuit is called potential difference, or p.d. Another name is "voltage" because p.d. is measured in volts. Ordinary flashlight batteries provide a voltage of about 1.5 volts; automobile batteries, 12 volts; and a domestic outlet for a lamp, about 110 volts (in many European countries it is 240 volts). Still higher voltages are used to send electricity across country from the generating plants to the factories, offices, and homes where it is used.

RESISTANCE

Most materials are neither perfect conductors nor perfect insulators. They *resist* the flow of current to a greater or lesser extent. A piece of wire included in a circuit to control the flow of current by its resistance is called a *resistor*. Resistance is measured in units called ohms. The greater the resistance of a component in a circuit, the more p.d. is needed to make a given current flow in it.

In a small pocket flashlight there may be a bulb with a resistance of about 3 ohms and two 1.5-volt batteries. (The total p.d. that can be delivered by a voltage source, such as a battery or generator, is called its electromotive force, or e.m.f.) The batteries are connected end-to-end so that their e.m.f.s add together to give a total voltage of about 3 volts. Current is measured in amperes—"amps" for short. The current in amps that will flow through the bulb is given by the e.m.f. in volts divided by the resistance in ohms, in this case 1 amp. (It is actually slightly less than that because the batteries and other components in the circuit also have some resistance.)

SERIES AND PARALLEL

The amount of current that will flow in a circuit depends not only on what components are connected into the circuit, but on the ways in which they are connected. In the diagram on the right, first one and then two identical batteries are used to light a bulb. Then the two batteries are used to light two bulbs. Current-measuring devices called ammeters are included in the circuits. The resistances of the batteries and the ammeters are so small that they can be ignored.

The bulbs are first connected in *series*—that is, so that the same current passes through both of them. Their resistances add, so that their combined resistance is twice the resistance of one of them. Less current flows in this case than when there is only one bulb in the circuit.

When the bulbs are connected in *parallel*, the current is split as it passes through them. There is the same voltage across each bulb, and it produces the same current in each bulb separately. The currents join as they flow out of the bulbs, so the combined current in the main part of the circuit is twice the current there would be if only one bulb were in the circuit. The combined resistance of the two bulbs in parallel is effectively half the resistance of each bulb singly.

VOLTAGE, RESISTANCE, AND CURRENT

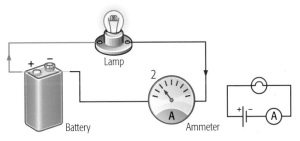

A battery and ammeter (for measuring current), both with zero resistance, are connected in series with a bulb so that the same current flows through all three. The ammeter shows that the current is 2 amps.

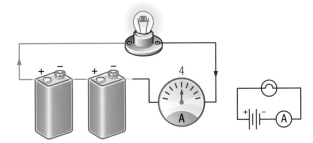

Two batteries in series give twice the potential difference across the bulb. Because the resistance in the circuit is unchanged, the current is now 4 amps.

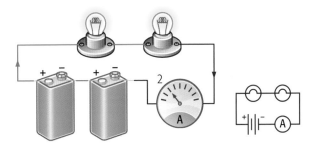

When two bulbs are connected in series their combined resistance is twice that of a single lamp. The current is halved to 2 amps.

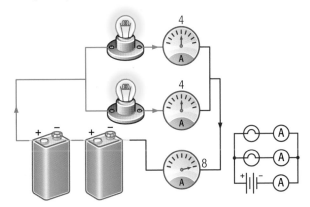

Two bulbs are connected in parallel, but each has the potential difference of two batteries across it, so a current of 4 amps again flows through each. The combined current is 8 amps.

Current and stored charge

To make use of electric current it is often necessary to measure it very accurately. A device for measuring current is called an ammeter. Nearly all measuring instruments make use of the current's magnetic properties. Often it is necessary to stop the flow of current and store charge in one place, in a device called a capacitor.

MANY CURRENT-MEASURING devices are based on the fact that an electric current sets up a magnetic field around itself. This field will move a nearby compass needle and push or pull a nearby wire carrying another current. If a wire is looped into a coil, it behaves like a magnet, with one end of the coil acting as the magnet's north pole and the other as the south pole. If such a coil is hung from a thread, and a current is passed through it, the coil will swing so that its poles are pointing north–south, just like the needle of a magnetic compass. The stronger the current flowing in the coil, the stronger the twisting force.

THE MOVING-COIL AMMETER

In the usual type of ammeter, or current-measuring device, the current flows through a coil that is wound around a core of soft iron (that is, nearly pure iron, rather than steel). The core "magnifies" the coil's field. The coil is suspended between the two poles of a strong permanent horseshoe-shaped magnet. When current flows the coil twists to line up with the permanent magnet's field, but the spring by which it is suspended resists this motion. The coil turns through a greater or smaller angle, depending on the strength of the current, which is indicated by a needle attached to the moving coil and a scale.

CHARGING A CAPACITOR

A battery transfers electrons from one plate of a capacitor to the other. Their mutual attraction holds the electrons there when the battery is removed. The plates discharge, causing an electric spark, when the wires are brought together.

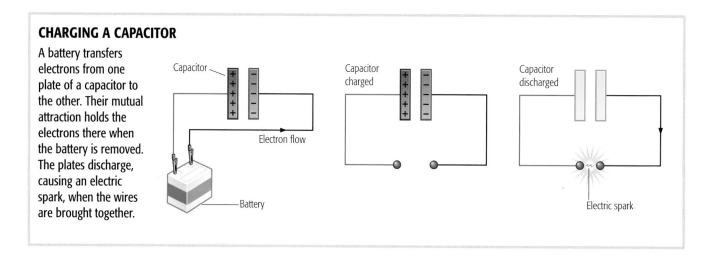

Capacitor

Electron flow

Battery

Capacitor charged

Capacitor discharged

Electric spark

THE GALVANOMETER

A very sensitive current-measuring device, which does not use a moving needle, is called a galvanometer. Again it uses a coil suspended in the magnetic field of a permanent magnet. It is also enclosed within a draft-excluding container with a window. The coil carries a mirror, which reflects a beam of light shone in through the window. As a current flows through the coil, the coil swings backward and forward through an angle that is larger for larger currents. Several meters away the beam leaving the window forms a spot of light that moves first one way and then the other through a long distance, making very accurate measurements possible.

STORING CHARGE

A capacitor can store electric charge. A highly simplified type consists of two parallel metal plates (see the illustration on the left). If they are connected to the two terminals of a battery, electrons pushed away from the negative terminal accumulate on one plate. Electrons are drawn away from the other plate by the attraction of the positive battery terminal. As electrons build up on the first plate they repel following electrons more and more strongly, and the current falls. Electrons flowing from the second plate toward the battery are held back by the attraction of the net positive charge remaining on that plate. The current falls to zero.

If the battery is removed, and the two ends of the wires from the plates stay unconnected, the electrons stay on one plate. But if the two wire ends are brought close together, the electrons can flow across the small air-gap to the other plate, attracted by the positive charges. There is now no net charge on either plate—the

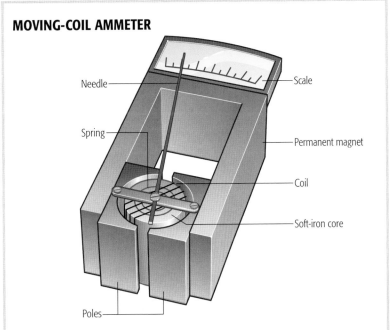

MOVING-COIL AMMETER

Needle — Scale

Spring

Permanent magnet

Coil

Soft-iron core

Poles

A current through the coil temporarily turns it into a magnet. Affected by the field of the permanent magnet, it rotates, moving the needle over a scale.

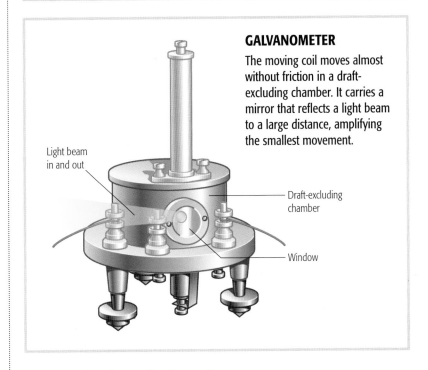

GALVANOMETER

The moving coil moves almost without friction in a draft-excluding chamber. It carries a mirror that reflects a light beam to a large distance, amplifying the smallest movement.

Light beam in and out

Draft-excluding chamber

Window

capacitor has been discharged.

Capacitors are important components of electrical circuits. One type consists of two long strips of metal foil, separated by a material called a dielectric and rolled up. The dielectric increases the amount of charge that can be stored.

☞ *See also* Direct and alternating **7** : 20; Potential difference **7** : 8; Producing charge **6** : 6

Resistance and power

The power needed to drive an electrical device, and the power that it can deliver, both depend crucially on its resistance, as well as on the voltage—that is, on the potential difference (p.d.)—applied across it. Designing an electrical device is largely a matter of putting the right amount of resistance in the right parts of its circuit.

A GERMAN PHYSICIST NAMED Georg Ohm made an important advance in the study of electricity in the early 19th century. He found that in many materials, especially metals, the current that flows through a given piece of the material—a piece of wire, for example—is proportional to the voltage across the material. That is, if a p.d. of 10 volts is applied, twice as much current will flow as when only 5 volts is applied, provided the temperature is kept constant.

No material follows this law exactly, but those that obey it approximately are sufficiently numerous to be very important and are called ohmic. The law can be written as

$$I = V/R$$

in which V is the p.d., I is the current, and R is simply the resistance of that particular piece of material. This equation can also be written in the

◁ **Keeping the lights burning**
Bulbs on a Christmas tree are usually connected in groups. The members of one group are in series with one another, but the group as a whole is in parallel with other groups. When one bulb blows, all the bulbs in that group go out, but most of the bulbs keep shining.

equivalent forms

$$V = IR$$

and

$$R = V/I$$

The flow of current through a resistive material generates heat. To keep the temperature constant the heat must be continually removed. As the temperature of a material is raised, its resistance usually increases, though again this is not true of all materials.

The resistance of a particular piece of material depends not only on what it is made of, but also on its shape. The resistance of a metal wire is much greater than the resistance of the same piece of metal melted down and formed into a shorter, fatter cylinder. For a given material, the resistance increases as length increases, and decreases as the cross-sectional area increases.

Resistors used in electrical and electronic circuits are made from metal wire or from carbon in a casing. They have their resistance marked on the casing in a code consisting of colored bands.

GEORG OHM

The German physicist Georg Ohm was born in the Bavarian city of Erlangen in 1787, where he studied at the university. He published his famous law in 1827, but its importance in bringing clarity to the study of electricity, in which ideas were still very confused, was not at first recognized. He became Director of the Polytechnic Institute of Nuremberg from 1833 until 1849, and from 1852 was Professor of Experimental Physics at the University of Munich. He died in 1854. By then the value of his law, which describes the behavior of a large class of materials, had become clear. By 1870 the unit of resistance had been named in his honor.

OHM'S LAW

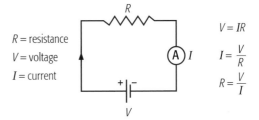

R = resistance
V = voltage
I = current

$$V = IR$$
$$I = \frac{V}{R}$$
$$R = \frac{V}{I}$$

Ohm's law states that, provided temperature is kept constant, the ratio of the p.d. across a conductor (V) to the current flowing through it (I) is a constant, the resistance (R). This can be written in the three forms shown at the right.

IN SERIES AND IN PARALLEL

Resistors can be arranged in different ways in a circuit to produce different effective combined resistances (see the diagram on page 16). Where two or more resistors are arranged in series so that the same current flows through all of them, their resistances add up. It needs a higher p.d. to drive a given current through them.

Alternatively, resistors can be arranged in parallel so that they have the same p.d. across them, but different currents flow through them. In this case the separate currents through the different resistors combine when they emerge. The parallel resistors effectively have a smaller resistance than any one of them does by itself.

If, for example, there are three resistors, R_1, R_2, and R_3, then the current through R_1 is V/R_1, and similarly for the other two. The combined current is

$$V/R_1 + V/R_2 + V/R_3$$

or

$$V(1/R_1 + 1/R_2 + 1/R_3)$$

This is the current that would be produced by a single resistance R if its value is given by the equation

$$1/R = 1/R_1 + 1/R_2 + 1/R_3$$

So R is the combined resistance of the three resistors when connected in parallel.

☞ *See also* Changing resistance **7** : 18; Semiconductor materials **9** : 16; Solid-state devices **9** : 20

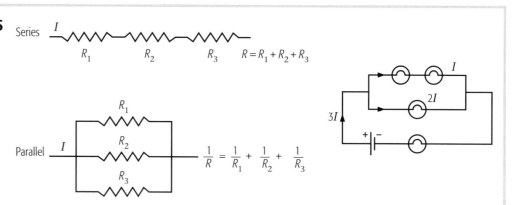
RESISTANCE AND HEATING

All the time a current flows through a material, it generates heat. It is put to work in electric ovens, irons, toasters, kettles, and water-heaters, in which current flowing through a wire makes that wire hot.

Electric light bulbs also work on the same principle. The tungsten filaments (wires) in light bulbs are designed to get so hot that they glow and give off light. These bulbs are described as "incandescent."

POWER AND ENERGY

Every electrical device requires energy to make it work. A great deal is needed by a water-heater, very little by a portable radio. The rate at which energy is used by a device is called its power consumption (power is the rate of expenditure of energy). In the electrical industry power is measured in units of watts (symbol W) or kilowatts (symbol kW). A kilowatt is equal to 1,000 watts. An ordinary incandescent bulb consumes about 100 W, a toaster typically uses 1 kW, and a television set about $\frac{1}{6}$ kW.

The amount of energy a device uses in a given time is found by multiplying its power consumption by the time. The unit used is the kilowatt-hour (also simply called a "unit"). It is the energy used by a 1-kW device running for 1 hour, or a 100-W device running for 10 hours.

Electricity consumers, whether in homes, offices, or factories, pay the generating companies for the amount of energy they use. A meter on the premises measures the energy used by measuring the amount of current going to the premises. The power used

ENERGY CONSUMPTION

The number of units of electrical energy typically used by various home appliances in 1 hour. The red circles show the energy usage in visual form.

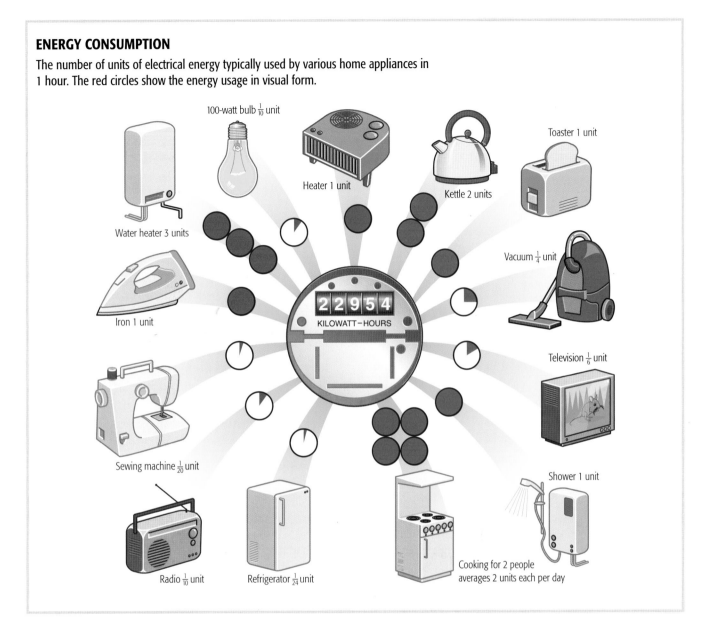

100-watt bulb $\frac{1}{10}$ unit

Heater 1 unit

Toaster 1 unit

Kettle 2 units

Water heater 3 units

Vacuum $\frac{1}{4}$ unit

Iron 1 unit

22954

KILOWATT−HOURS

Television $\frac{1}{6}$ unit

Sewing machine $\frac{1}{20}$ unit

Shower 1 unit

Radio $\frac{1}{10}$ unit

Refrigerator $\frac{1}{24}$ unit

Cooking for 2 people averages 2 units each per day

is the current multiplied by the voltage at which it is supplied. It is continually measured and added up to give the total energy used.

VANISHING RESISTANCE

Some materials lose all their electrical resistance, becoming *superconductive*, when they are cooled sufficiently. This was discovered in 1911 by a Dutch physicist, Heike Kamerlingh Onnes, who found that the metal mercury becomes superconductive when its temperature is less than 4 degrees above absolute zero. Other materials show the same phenomenon at various low temperatures. From 1986 new materials were developed that show superconductivity at much higher temperatures, around 100 degrees K above absolute zero. If superconductivity at ordinary temperatures could be achieved, very cheap power transmission would become possible because very little energy would be lost from heating the transmission lines. Very fast computers could be built, and many other sophisticated new devices would become generally available.

Changing resistance

All electrical components in a circuit have some resistance, but this is not merely an inconvenience. It can be put to good use by engineers to provide us with heat and light, and to make electrical and electronic devices work in just the right way.

THE HEAT GENERATED when an electric current flows is caused by the current overcoming the resistance of the material through which it is flowing. The material contains imperfections and irregularities in its crystal structure, and they disturb the motion of the electrons. The more perfect a crystal is—the fewer the imperfections in its array of atoms—the less resistance it has because electrons can flow through it freely. The heating caused by a current flowing through a material with electrical resistance is called resistive heating.

The main use of resistive heating is in electric lighting. An electric bulb contains a metal filament, usually made of tungsten, which glows white-hot as current flows through it. The voltage from the power supply is (approximately) 110 volts in the United States. The power used up and converted into heat and light by a typical domestic light bulb is 100 watts, though bulbs with power consumption ranging from 10 watts to 150 watts are available. The more power that is used, the hotter and brighter the filament becomes.

The power (W) used by a bulb or any other device is equal to the current (I) that flows through it multiplied by the voltage (V) across it; in symbols,

$$W = IV$$

So a 100-watt bulb operated at 110 volts draws about 0.9 amps.

THE RHEOSTAT

Current passes from terminal A through the part of the coil of resistance wire between the contact and terminal B. As the contact is slid to the right, the current passes through less wire and hence experiences less resistance.

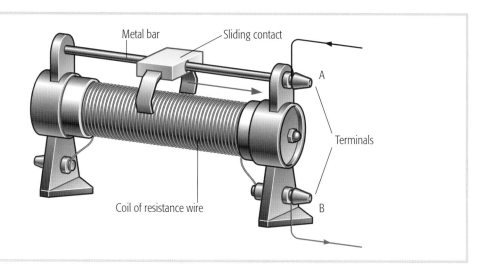

Metal bar — Sliding contact

A

Terminals

Coil of resistance wire

B

The resistance of the filament needed to produce this current from this voltage is

$$R = V/I = 110/0.9$$

which is approximately 120 ohms. A smaller resistance allows a larger current to flow, generating more power and making a brighter bulb.

A metal filament raised to the temperatures of thousands of degrees at which light bulbs have to operate would burn up in a moment as the metal combined with oxygen in the air. That is prevented by filling the bulb with an inert (unreactive) gas such as argon or krypton. The filament lasts much longer, although it will gradually lose atoms that are driven off by the high temperature. They coat the inside of the bulb, slightly dimming it. This effect is reduced in quartz-halogen lamps, in which the bulb glass contains quartz, and the gases in the bulb include halogens such as bromine. Chemical reactions in the bulb return tungsten atoms to the filament as fast as they are lost, so the filaments have a very long life.

The resistance of the various components of electrical devices must be precisely controlled in their construction in order to make the devices work properly. Some resistances must be variable. The volume control knob on traditional radio and TV sets works by increasing or decreasing the amount of resistance in the speaker circuit. The knob operates a rheostat, in which a contact slides over a coil of wire, altering the length of wire that the current flows through. The more wire the current flows through, the greater the resistance, and the current is diminished accordingly. Rheostats are also used in dimmer switches that control the lighting of a room or of an instrument display in a car dashboard or bedside radio.

△ **Incandescent lighting**
A tungsten filament glows white-hot as it is heated to thousands of degrees by an electric current passing through it.

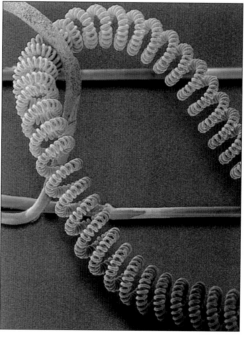

◁ **Coiled coil**
A magnified photograph of an electric light bulb's filament shows that it consists of a coil that is coiled again. This structure packs a great length of wire into minimal space.

☞ *See also* Producing heat **3** : 8; Producing light **4** : 6; Resistance and power **7** : 14

Direct and alternating

Once, electricity was supplied to homes and factories as one-way direct current. Now, all outlet current is AC, reversing its direction constantly. This is necessary to make power controllable, so that it can be delivered at the voltages that are needed.

THE ELECTRICITY THAT is supplied by utility companies to homes, offices, and industrial plant is not only at a much higher voltage than the electricity supplied by batteries in a portable radio or flashlight. It also differs in another crucial way. The current from a battery is *direct current*, or DC: it flows in one direction. The current from the regional power grid repeatedly changes its direction. This is called *alternating current*, or AC.

Alternating current has immense advantages over direct current for large-scale uses. AC current has strong magnetic effects, which are vital to a host of electrical devices. And related to this is the fact that AC voltage can be altered readily, but DC voltage cannot. Different voltages are needed for different purposes. AC voltages are also easily produced by turbine generators.

CHANGING VOLTAGES

Every electric current generates a magnetic field. If wire is looped into a coil, the whole coil behaves like a bar magnet (see pages 12–13). An AC current generates an alternating magnetic field.

An electric current can also be generated by a magnetic field, but only by a changing one. Moving a bar magnet near a wire causes a voltage to develop along the wire while the field is changing. The changing field *induces* a voltage. If the wire is looped into a coil of many turns, the voltage

◁ **Transforming power**
Large transformers at an electricity substation step down the voltage of the supply from the large voltages of the long-distance supply to the voltages used in factories or in homes.

DC AND AC

A battery delivers a one-way voltage that is steady. This produces a constant one-way current. It is called DC, or direct current. The graph of voltage against time is a horizontal straight line. Turbines in power plants deliver a voltage that constantly reverses in direction, creating an alternating current, or AC. The voltage–time graph then has a wavelike shape.

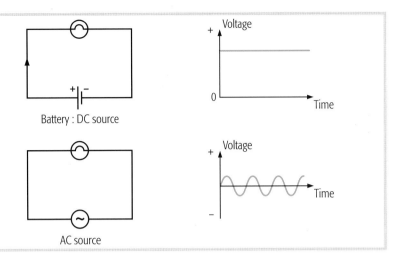

Battery : DC source

AC source

is generated across each turn of the coil, and the cumulative voltage across the whole coil is increased.

This makes it possible to alter AC voltages easily. AC current flows through a coil in one circuit, called the primary circuit. The coil is wound around an iron core, which also passes through the coil of the secondary circuit. The magnetic field generated by the primary coil creates a bigger magnetic field in the iron. This field fills the interior of the iron and passes through the secondary coil. Because the field is varying in strength and direction, it induces an AC voltage in each loop of the secondary coil. The more loops there are in the secondary coil, the bigger the voltage that develops.

If there are fewer turns in the secondary coil than in the primary coil, a smaller voltage is developed in the secondary than in the primary.

This device is called a transformer. Transformers are used to step up the voltage of current from a power station to transmit over long-distance high-voltage lines. Other transformers, housed in unmanned installations called substations, are placed near industrial plant and near residential areas to step down voltages.

HOW A TRANSFORMER WORKS

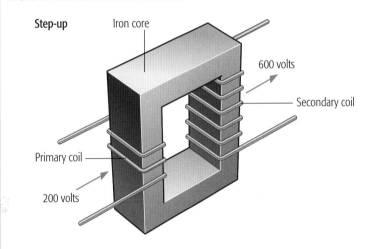

The alternating magnetic field of the primary coil is channeled through the secondary coil by the iron core. The secondary has more turns and develops a higher voltage.

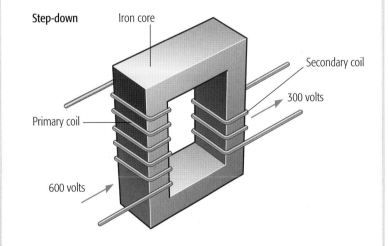

When the secondary coil has fewer turns than the primary, it develops a lower voltage, making the setup into a step-down transformer.

☞ See also Electric batteries **6** : 42; Electricity from machines **7** : 22; Electricity in the home **7** : 30

Electricity from machines

An electricity-generating plant is a place where energy of motion is turned into electrical energy. Monster machines and huge amounts of fuel are needed. With each year that passes, the electricity-supply industry is called on to deliver more energy to the expanding industries of the world.

IN A POWER plant turbines are spun by steam to generate electricity. The steam has to be produced by boiling purified water circulating in a closed system of pipes. Plants differ in the source of the heat they use to boil the water. Some burn coal; others, oil or gas; still others use heat from a nuclear reactor. A few use alternative forms of energy, such as sunlight or wave power, or heat from rocks deep beneath the ground.

The steam used in a conventional or nuclear power plant is superheated to temperatures of 550°C (1,000°F) or more. This steam is forced into the turbine, which consists of rotors, sets of rotating wheels equipped with fan blades, alternating with sets of fixed fan blades called stators. The steam's pressure forces the turbine's shaft to spin. The steam's temperature and pressure fall, but it is then led through lower-pressure stages of the turbine to extract as much energy as possible.

The last of the steam's heat is removed as it is circulated through pipes that are cooled by water from some external source such as a lake or river. The condensed water is returned to be heated again. The cooling water is returned to its source, though its possible effect on the environment must be carefully monitored and minimized. Warm water encourages the growth of algae, for example, which can cut down the oxygen available to fish. Clouds of water vapor can often be seen rising from the cooling towers that are a feature of many power plants.

THE TURBOGENERATOR

From the steam turbine runs a shaft that spins at 3,600 rpm (in the United States) and is part of the generator. There is a strong magnetic field in the generator, which is produced by an

MICHAEL FARADAY

The discoverer of electromagnetic induction, Michael Faraday, has a host of discoveries in physics and chemistry to his name. He had attracted notice from an early age. Born the son of a blacksmith in 1791, he was largely self-educated. At the age of 21 he made notes of lectures on chemistry given by Sir Humphry Davy and showed them to Davy, who was so impressed that he gave the young man a job as his assistant. Faraday discovered new chemical compounds, including benzene; he cooled gases until they liquefied; he investigated electromagnetism—discovering the dynamo effect (page 26)—and the chemical effects of electricity. He also investigated the effects of magnetism on light. On his death in 1867 he was recognized as perhaps the greatest scientific experimenter of all time. His discovery of electromagnetic induction laid the foundations for the electricity industry that was soon to develop.

independent supply of current flowing through electric coils called field windings. A complex structure called an armature, carrying electrical coils, spins in this magnetic field. An electromotive force of about 25,000 volts is generated.

Because the shaft rotates at 3,600 rpm, the current alternates at 60 Hz (that is, 60 hertz, or 60 times per second). This means that during 1/120 second the number of electrons flowing in one direction increases and then decreases to zero; and then during the next 1/120 second the flow builds up to a maximum in the reverse direction and then decreases to zero again. It is an alternating current (AC).

STEPPING UP

The power is delivered from the generator at about 25,000 volts. It is sent to a transformer, which steps up the voltage to several hundred thousand volts. This is necessary for sending power over long distances. The electrical cables have resistance, and heat is generated in them, which

◁ **Turboalternator**
Steam-driven turbines called turboalternators generate electricity. The main energy sources are coal, oil, gas, and nuclear energy.

☞ *See also* Direct and alternating **7** : 20; Electricity in the home **7** : 30; Producing large charges **6** : 18

is wasted. Having a very high voltage driving a low current can minimize the heat lost.

The high-tension ("tension" here just means voltage) lines fan out from the plant in all directions to cities and towns in the area it serves.

These voltages are extremely dangerous, and the wires must be carried on tall towers well off the ground. They need extra support where they pass over highways. Insulators keep the current-carrying wires separated from the towers on which they are supported. In some places high-tension cables are carried in pipes buried underground.

STEPPING DOWN

Near an area where there are factories or other industrial plants, power cables lead to an unmanned substation. Here transformers reduce the voltages. A variety of different voltages are produced to meet the needs of different users. The substation runs automatically. It is securely fenced off because it is dangerous for any unauthorized person to wander into it.

△ **Feeding the demand**
Power plants demand
an endless supply of fuel.
Here a huge train of
railroad cars carries coal
to a generating plant,
recognizable by its
cooling towers.

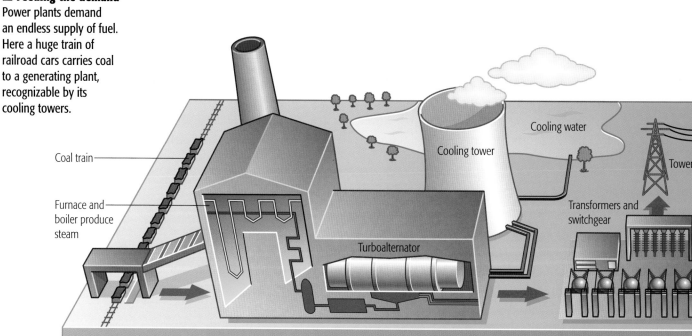

Coal train

Furnace and
boiler produce
steam

Turboalternator

Cooling water

Cooling tower

Transformers and
switchgear

Towers

Where power is to be delivered to homes, the voltage is finally reduced to about 110 volts (in the United States; about 240 volts in some other countries). The power is brought to an individual home along an overhead cable or under the street.

AC AND DC GENERATORS

When a coil of wire rotates in a magnetic field the current in it is automatically AC. Think about what happens on one side of a single coil: the current in it alternately flows along it one way and then the opposite way because that side of the coil moves through the magnetic field one way in one half of its revolution and the other way in the other half. AC current can then be drawn from the coil by having a terminal of the external circuit that is permanently connected to each side of the coil (see the left-hand illustration at the top of page 27 for the principle).

Sometimes it is advantageous to produce DC current. In this case the connections to the generator have to be more complicated. The two terminals of the rotating coil can be in the form of the two halves of a split ring. They make contact alternately with one terminal of the external circuit and then the other (see the right-hand illustration at the top of page 27). This reverses the connection at the moment the voltage in the rotating coil reverses. The current in the external circuit is DC, though it changes in strength during each rotation of the coil.

Practical generators have to be much more complicated than this. There is a set of rotating coils, and current is drawn only from the coil that is experiencing a peak voltage at that moment. The magnetic field is provided by an electromagnet—that is, it is generated by current flowing in special coils.

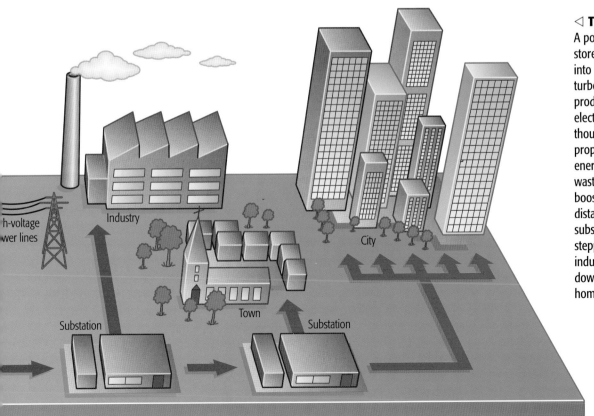

h-voltage
wer lines

Industry

City

Substation

Town

Substation

◁ **The supply chain**
A power plant converts the stored energy of its fuel into steam, which a turboalternator uses to produce a supply of electric current at tens of thousands of volts. A high proportion of the fuel's energy is inevitably lost as waste heat. Transformers boost the voltage for long-distance transmission. At substations the voltage is stepped down to supply industry and stepped down still further to supply homes and offices.

MOTION INTO ELECTRICITY

A dynamo can be used on a bicycle to power the lights. The turning of the wheel rotates the shaft, which generates DC current in the coils. Often the dynamo supplies a battery, which smoothes the current going to the bicycle lights.

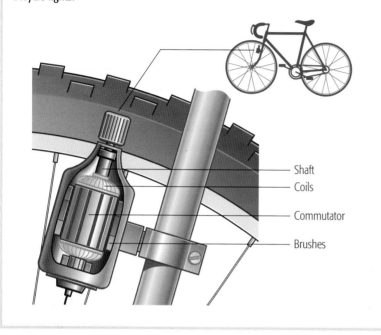

Shaft
Coils
Commutator
Brushes

POWER FROM THE WIND

A wind turbine has blades shaped as carefully as the propeller or wings of an airplane to extract maximum energy from the wind. A gearbox ensures the generator is driven at the optimum speed whatever the speed of the blade. The turbine's blades may be 5 meters (about 15ft) from tip to tip. "Wind farms" of hundreds of turbines exist in some areas, including California.

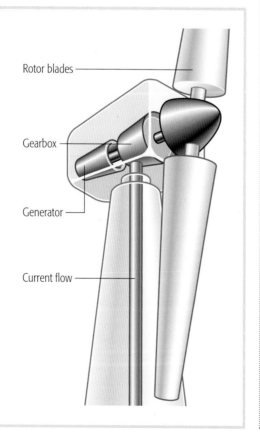

Rotor blades

Gearbox

Generator

Current flow

Many people are concerned about our use of fossil fuels—coal, oil, and gas—because mining and burning them pollutes the environment, and because there are only limited reserves of them. They fear nuclear energy even more because of the problem of disposing of radioactive waste and the possibility of a serious accident that would release radioactivity into the atmosphere. They look to sunlight, the wind, waves, tides, and geothermal energy as clean and unlimited alternatives.

Large clusters of wind turbines are a common sight in the windy, low-lying regions of the Netherlands, Denmark, and other northern European countries, and there are also many in California. The electricity is generated in the wind turbine itself. A large machine in favorable conditions can generate around 400 kW. A very large "wind farm" generates as much power as a conventional power plant. But output is very variable, since it depends on weather conditions.

Wave-power machines extract energy from the bobbing motion of sea waves. They are located about 2 kilometers (over a mile) off the coast. The waves' motion may be used to pump air into reservoirs from which it can be released gradually to drive generators. Or it may be used to rock mechanical devices whose nodding motion is converted into electrical energy. Wave machines are unobtrusive and ideal for use wherever waves are consistently strong.

Solar energy can be turned into electricity in two ways. A large field of mirrors can be used to reflect sunlight onto a boiler, producing steam that drives a turbine in the ordinary way. Large installations in the Mojave Desert use thousands of mirrors to focus sunlight onto a vessel containing

PRINCIPLE OF AC AND DC GENERATORS

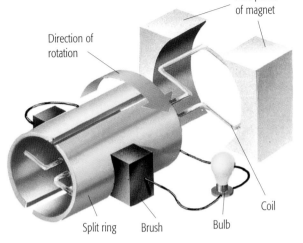

Direction of rotation

Pole pieces of magnet

Coil

Commutator

Brushes

Bulb

In an AC generator each side of the coil is always in contact with the same terminal, so that an AC current is delivered.

Direction of rotation

Pole pieces of magnet

Coil

Split ring

Brush

Bulb

In this simplified DC generator split-ring commutators convert the AC voltage from the rotating coil into a DC current.

a molten salt. The salt's stored heat is used to boil water and make high-pressure steam.

The other method of converting sunlight to electricity is to allow it to shine onto a photoelectric material, which directly generates a current. Photoelectric cells are frequently made from semiconducting materials such as silicon. On a small scale such photoelectric cells are used in solar-powered devices such as calculators. Photocells convert about 15 percent of the sunlight's energy into electrical energy. They produce DC current, which has to be converted into AC for large-scale use.

In some American states the electricity supply is deregulated. Consumers choose which energy company they will pay, and that company accordingly generates more electricity to go into the supply. The difference to the consumer is in the prices that the companies charge and also in the methods of generation they use. Some companies supply "green" electricity generated from "renewable" sources such as hydroelectricity, wind

PRACTICAL AC GENERATOR

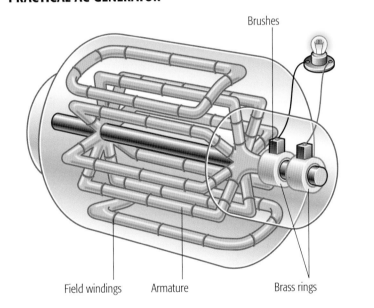

Brushes

Field windings

Armature

Brass rings

The generators in power plants are driven by steam turbines. There is a set of rotating coils, which collectively are called the armature, and the magnetic field is provided by electric current flowing through coils called the field windings. The rings draw current from the coil in which the strongest current is flowing at that moment.

power, or solar energy, and consumers can express their preference for such sources by buying their electricity from those companies.

Electricity at work

Electricity is industry's workhorse in countless ways, operating switches, transmitting information, and carrying data in instruments and computers. There is a vast range of ways of generating it too, although "alternative" technology cannot yet rival the methods employed in conventional power plants.

THE HEAT THAT electric currents can generate is used to good effect in many industries. High temperatures are needed to refine iron, freeing it from impurities, and in making steel by adding controlled amounts of other materials to iron. Electric furnaces are important in this industry.

In smaller furnaces a current is passed through heating coils around the furnace. In the electric arc furnace carbon electrodes are suspended above the metal that is to be melted. A high voltage applied to each electrode in rapid succession causes an electric arc to be struck between the electrode and the metal—that is, an electric spark jumps across the gap between them, and current flows through the metal, heating it.

In the induction furnace, rapidly varying AC currents flow in coils outside the furnace. The varying magnetic field they generate penetrates the metal in the furnace and induces current in it, as in a transformer (see pages 20–21). The current heats the metal and melts it.

Electric current has numerous other uses, not only in steelmaking but in all other industries as well. Hoists, drills, and lathes are all operated by electric motors. Electromagnetic cranes can also lift heavy loads. They contain powerful electromagnets consisting of an iron core with a current-carrying electric coil wound around it. As long as the current flows, the device is a powerful magnet capable of lifting heavy loads of metallic materials.

SOLAR POWER

Scientists and engineers everywhere are working hard to exploit the potential of photoelectric cells. These cells are already indispensable in spacecraft, which can be powered for many years by sunlight, which in space is uninterrupted and undimmed

▽ **Electric furnace**
This molten steel being poured into molds was produced in an electric furnace. Such furnaces may use AC or DC power, and large ones can produce 150 tons of steel in an hour.

SOLAR POWER

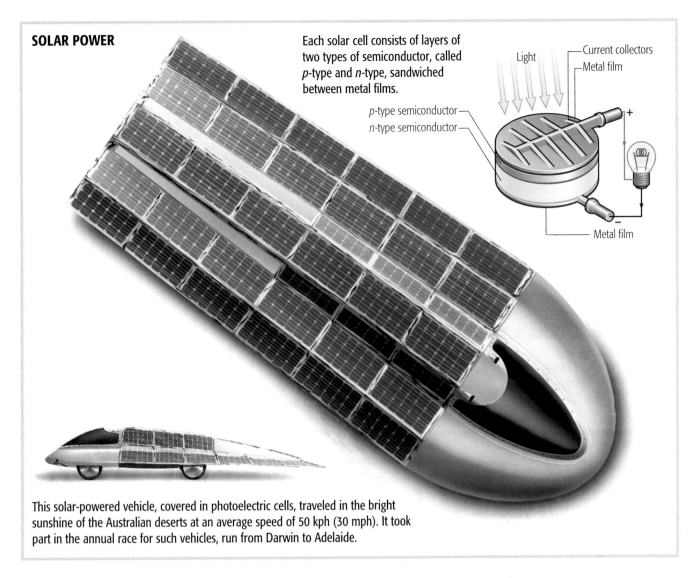

Each solar cell consists of layers of two types of semiconductor, called *p*-type and *n*-type, sandwiched between metal films.

Light

Current collectors
Metal film

p-type semiconductor
n-type semiconductor

+

−

Metal film

This solar-powered vehicle, covered in photoelectric cells, traveled in the bright sunshine of the Australian deserts at an average speed of 50 kph (30 mph). It took part in the annual race for such vehicles, run from Darwin to Adelaide.

by Earth's hazy or cloudy atmosphere.

Experimental vehicles have been developed that run on solar energy alone. Many of them compete in an annual race from north to south across Australia. Winners have reached speeds of 80 kph (50 mph), but this is under exceptionally favorable conditions and with machines that are swathed in solar cells and highly streamlined.

Practical electric cars might be built, but using batteries rather than solar energy. If batteries that were more compact, lighter, and capable of storing more energy could be developed, electric cars might rival gasoline-driven cars for city use.

When the car's batteries were nearly run down, the driver would go to a resupply point—perhaps at an ordinary gas station—and exchange the old batteries for new, freshly charged ones.

The future might lie with a radical alternative to the battery called a fuel cell. It generates electricity from chemical reactions, as do batteries, but with the difference that the chemicals are supplied continuously from outside. Many types have been developed, using a variety of fuels, including hydrogen, methane, and carbon monoxide, reacting with air. Often the only waste product is water.

☞ *See also* Electricity in the home **7** : 30; Talking along wires **7** : 34; Talking through the air **7** : 38

Electricity in the home

The ordinary person's home was revolutionized by the arrival of electricity during the 20th century. Light and warmth (or coolness) were instantly available any hour of the day or night. A host of domestic aids—washing machines, dishwashers, air-conditioners, and vacuum cleaners—were made possible by electricity.

THE VOLTAGE AT which electricity needs to be supplied for home appliances is high enough to be dangerous. So it must be provided safely and in such a way that flaws and human error do not lead to disastrous results.

CIRCUIT WIRING

In many homes each room or floor is served by a pair of wires, called a circuit, consisting of a live wire (red) and a neutral wire (black). Lights and low-power appliances have a "single-pole" switch in the live wire only. High-power appliances use "double-pole" switches, which interrupt both wires. Each circuit leads from the fusebox, in which a common kind of fuse is the screw-in type (below).

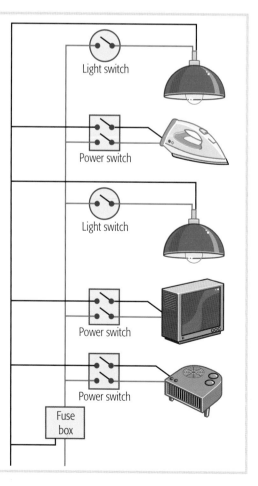

Light switch

Power switch

Light switch

Power switch

Power switch

Fuse box

Screw-type (plug) fuse

A modern American domestic supply normally delivers at least 200 amps, and possibly 440 amps or more. The electricity supply is described as being at 110 or 120 volts. Both are "nominal" values—127 volts is a typical true value, and voltage may be varied slightly at different times by supply companies. Usually a home receives a "three-wire service," via two "hot" wires and a "neutral" one. A circuit connected to one of the hot wires delivers a supply of about 120 volts; one that is connected to both delivers a supply of about 240 volts for the modern devices that require the higher voltage.

The supply is connected to the home's system through a power box, or fusebox. It contains either circuit breakers or fuses. A fuse contains a piece of wire that is designed to melt and break if too much current flows through it. A circuit breaker is a switch that automatically cuts off the current in a circuit if the current rises too high. A current surge is an indication that electricity may be dangerously leaking from some appliance. A circuit breaker can be reset when the problem has been corrected, but a "blown" fuse has to be replaced with a new one.

RING CIRCUIT
The wiring to each room or floor leads from the fusebox, goes around all the power outlets, and then returns to the fusebox. An appliance that consumes a lot of power, such as a stove or water-heater, has its own circuit, leading directly from the fusebox.

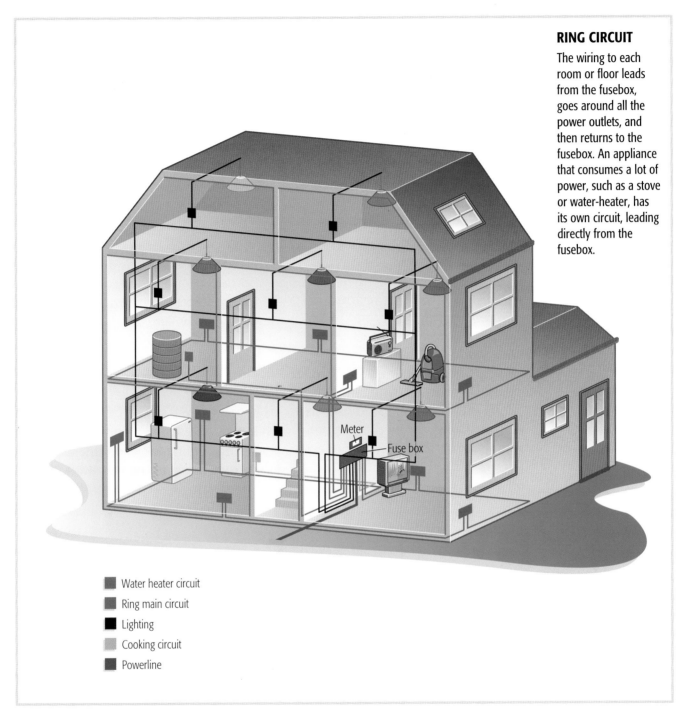

Meter

Fuse box

- Water heater circuit
- Ring main circuit
- Lighting
- Cooking circuit
- Powerline

Inside the home appliances are connected to the supply via two or three wires. One is called the *hot* or *live* line, while the second, along which the current returns, is called the *neutral* line. There is often a third wire, called the *ground* wire. It connects the casing of the device, such as a desk lamp or a TV set, to a ground wire in the household circuit that is ultimately connected, via the control box, to a metal rod sunk into the earth. If a flaw should arise, and the casing of the appliance suddenly came into contact with a high voltage, current would flow along the ground wire rather than into the body of a person touching the "live" object because of the low resistance of the ground wire and of the earth itself.

☞ *See also* Electricity from machines **7** : 22; Producing heat **3** : 8; Producing light **4** : 6

Messages along wires

Faraday's discovery that an electric current has magnetic effects was soon applied to long-distance communication. Around 1837 the electric telegraph was invented in England and the United States. By 1900 telegraph wires girdled the Earth.

THE ELECTRIC TELEGRAPH was devised independently in the United States by the artist and inventor Samuel Morse, and in England by the physicist Charles Wheatstone and the engineer William Cooke. In Morse's system an operator pressed a key to allow short or long bursts of current to flow in a wire. At the other end the magnetic field of the current operated a device that made short or long marks on a roll of paper. This automatic recording system was discarded when operators found they could recognize the messages being sent from the sound of the apparatus alone. Morse developed a code in which "dots" and "dashes" (short and long pulses) represented letters and numerals.

SPANNING THE OCEANS

In 1843 Cooke and Wheatstone set up the first public telegraph line along a railroad line running westward from London. In 1844 Morse sent the

▷ **Cable across the Atlantic Ocean**
The giant steamship *Great Eastern* laid the first successful telegraph cable across the Atlantic in 1866. An earlier cable had failed after operating for only a short time.

message "What hath God wrought!" from Washington, D.C. to Baltimore, Maryland, along a line built with government money. Telegraph lines rapidly spread across North America and Europe, revolutionizing commerce and warfare.

The telegraph developed into the teleprinter, in which a message could be typed in on a typewriter-style keyboard and was automatically typed out at the receiver. However, the teleprinter has been superseded by e-mail and by fax.

Fax (facsimile) transmission is the sending of an image of a document over telephone lines (a telephone "line" including not just wires but radio links). The document is scanned line by line, and the pattern of light and dark spots is converted into electrical pulses. At the receiver the pulses are converted back into spots for printing so that the image is reassembled on paper.

INTERNATIONAL MORSE CODE

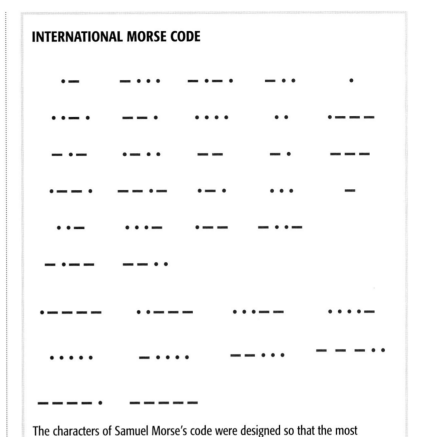

The characters of Samuel Morse's code were designed so that the most frequently occurring letters were the shortest and quickest to send.

FAX MACHINE

When a fax machine transmits, the document being sent is wound through the machine, and an array of light sensors converts the image on the paper into a sequence of electronic impulses which are transmitted over an ordinary telephone line. When the machine receives, it winds heat-sensitive paper past an array of elements, each of which is briefly heated at the right moments to make dark marks on the paper. Other types of fax machine use plain paper. The keypad is used for dialing telephone numbers.

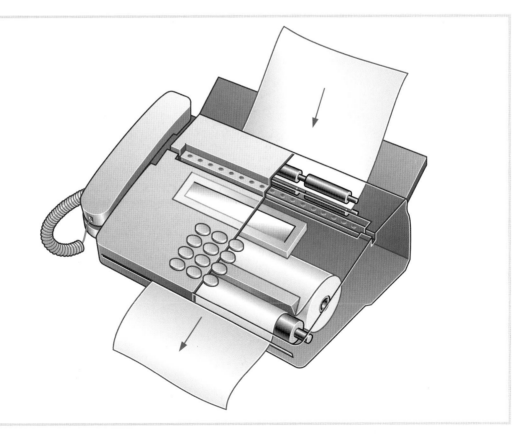

☞ *See also* **Talking along wires 7** : 34; **Messages through the air 7** : 36; **Talking through the air 7** : 38

Talking along wires

Anyone who has a phone can call any other phone user in the world by pushing a sequence of buttons. The connection is made without the involvement of any other human being. Most phone calls are still carried by wires, though often with part of the connection being provided by radio links.

MODERN TELEPHONE HANDSETS work in much the same way as the first successful telephone ever built, which was made by the Scots-born American inventor Alexander Graham Bell in 1877. The sound of the speaker's voice, which consists of vibrations of the air, strikes a diaphragm, a thin piece of plastic. In one type of

▽ **Keeping the lines open**
A lineman climbs a telephone pole to carry out repairs. Electrical insulators shield the wires from the pole to prevent current leaking down it to the ground.

mouthpiece the plastic presses against a mass of carbon granules. A weak DC current supplied from the exchange passes through the carbon. As the constantly changing pressure of the air from the speaker's voice acts on the diaphragm, the diaphragm exerts a varying pressure on the granules. That affects the degree to which the granules are compressed, which in turn affects how easily an electric current can flow through the granules. The result is that a constantly varying electric current flows through the mouthpiece. In another type of mouthpiece the diaphragm moves an iron "pole piece" mounted inside a coil of wire. The moving iron causes variations in the electric current passing through the coil.

The weak varying current that emerges from the mouthpiece is an electrical copy of the pattern of sound waves that struck the mouthpiece. It travels over wires to the distant phone, where it is passed through the earpiece. It then flows through a coil forming an electromagnet. The fluctuating magnetic field that it sets up pulls on a metal diaphragm, making it vibrate in a pattern that is a copy of the original sound vibrations.

THE TELEPHONE NETWORK

Automatic equipment routes a phone call first to a local office, or exchange, and then through one or more long-distance offices. Finally it goes via the local office serving the person called to that person's telephone.

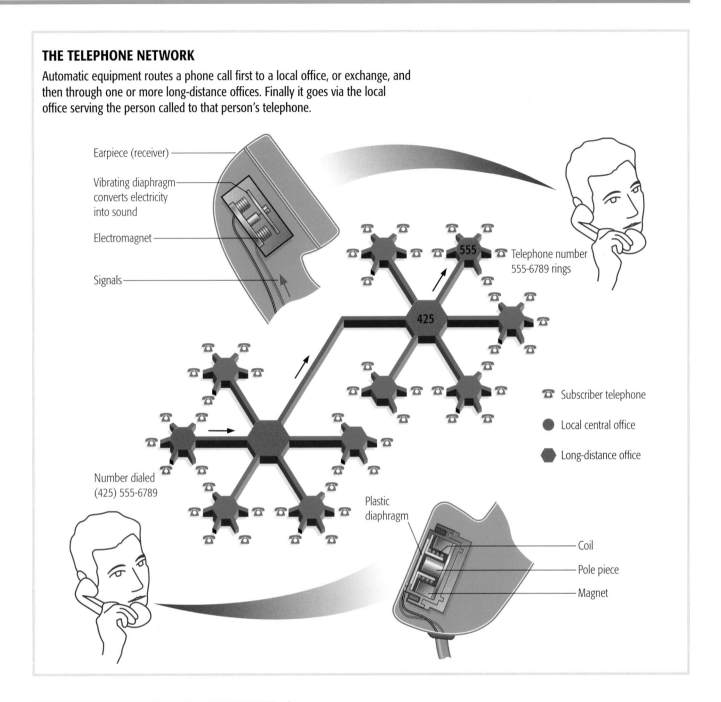

Earpiece (receiver)

Vibrating diaphragm converts electricity into sound

Electromagnet

Signals

Telephone number 555-6789 rings

555

425

Number dialed (425) 555-6789

☎ Subscriber telephone

● Local central office

⬡ Long-distance office

Plastic diaphragm

Coil

Pole piece

Magnet

ROUTING THE SIGNALS

In the earliest days of the telephone a caller would first ring their local telephone exchange. An operator would then connect the caller by pushing the two ends of a wire into the two sockets corresponding to the caller and the person called.

The first automatic telephone dialing systems used a dial, which was rotated with the finger, sending a series of pulses along the line. The pulses controlled the movements of a mechanical arm that rotated and moved vertically to set up the right connection. Phones are now equipped with push buttons. Pressing a button may send a series of pulses, as the old rotary dials did, or it may send audible tones that represent the numbers. The numbers that a caller dials provide an exact "route map" showing how the call must be switched to get to the right receiver.

☞ *See also* **Messages along wires 7** : 32; **Talking through the air 7** : 38; **Pictures through the air 7** : 42

Messages through the air

The next great leap forward was to communicate at a distance without wires. Within 70 years radio communication developed from the dots and dashes of Morse code to high-quality stereophonic transmissions of voice and music.

IN THE 1860s the British physicist James Clerk Maxwell predicted the existence of electromagnetic radiation—waves that consist of rapidly varying interlinked electric and magnetic fields. Movements of electric charge, he said, would cause these waves. He also said that they would travel at the speed of light. Indeed, Maxwell identified visible light, together with infrared radiation and ultraviolet radiation, as electromagnetic radiation of particular wavelengths. At that time radiations of shorter or longer wavelengths had yet to be discovered.

In 1886 some of those unknown radiations were observed. A German physicist, Heinrich Hertz, found that an electric spark sends out radiations. He could detect their effects with a coil of wire located some distance from the spark. The coil had a gap between its ends. As electromagnetic waves that were generated by a series of sparks passed through the coil, they induced an electromotive force—a voltage—in the coil, making sparks jump across the gap. Hertz had, in fact, sent the first radio signal. Experiments showed that the radiation traveled at the speed of light and had a wavelength much longer than that of light.

The Italian inventor Guglielmo Marconi developed radio into a practical form of "wireless telegraphy." Within six years of his first transmission he had sent signals in

◁ **The ears of the world**
These mesh dishes on a radio mast send and receive tightly focused radio beams at microwave wavelengths. The signals may be radio broadcasts, telephone conversations, or computer data.

WIRELESS TELEGRAPHY

Marconi made wireless transmission practical. He designed an improved *oscillator,* the circuit that generates high-frequency AC current. He let the AC current flow through a metal *antenna*, which sent out the electromagnetic radiation. He used a telegraph operator's key to generate bursts of current in the sending circuit. Marconi also improved the receiver so that it could detect signals better and *amplify* (strengthen) them. Eventually a loudspeaker was added.

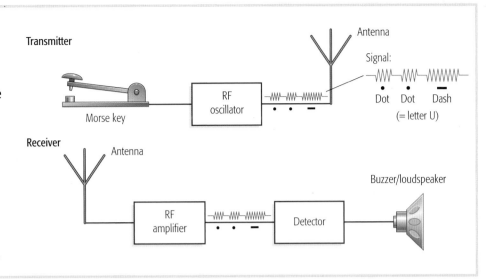

MIRRORS IN THE SKY

Radio waves of long, medium, and short wavelengths are reflected around the world from layers of ions–the ionosphere–high in the atmosphere. VHF (very high frequency) and UHF (ultrahigh frequency) waves penetrate the layers and are then relayed by artificial satellites orbiting beyond the atmosphere.

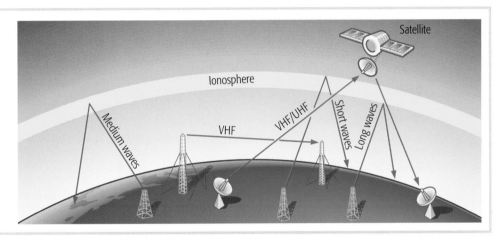

Morse code across the Atlantic. Other experimenters succeeded in transmitting the sounds of voices and music by radio. In 1920 the first public radio station began regular broadcasts from Pittsburgh, Pennsylvania.

Since then, broadcasting has spread to ever-higher frequencies. Today's VHF (very high frequency) and UHF (ultrahigh frequency) broadcasts use frequencies hundreds or thousands of times higher than those of Marconi. Enormous numbers of channels can be broadcast at these high frequencies, and better signal quality can be achieved. Achieving these higher frequencies was a matter of inventing better electronic circuits to control the electric currents involved.

GUGLIELMO MARCONI

Marconi was born of an Italian father and Irish mother in 1874. He made his first experiments in wireless telegraphy in his native country, Italy, but on patenting his system in Britain, he formed the Marconi Wireless Telegraph Co. in London. In 1896 he transmitted signals over 1.5 km (1 mile); soon he had sent signals from the shore to a ship 29 km (18 miles) away. In 1899 he set up regular communication between England and France. Marconi then attempted to send radio waves from England to Canada. Most scientists assumed that radio waves must travel in straight lines and would not be able to reach places over the horizon. To their astonishment, Marconi succeeded. He shared the 1909 Nobel Prize for Physics and worked on short-wave radio for the Italian government during World War I (1914–18). He died in 1937.

☞ *See also* Talking along wires **7** : 34; Talking through the air **7** : 38; Pictures through the air **7** : 42

Talking through the air

We can hear sounds from around the world whenever we want to at any time of the day or night. A microphone changes the sounds into patterns of electric currents, which are then translated into patterns of electromagnetic radiation—radio waves—that travel around the globe. The last step is to translate the electrical signals back into sounds.

THE ADVANCE FROM sending Morse code signals to transmitting the sounds of voices or music by radio (radiotelephony) involved several major steps. Wireless telegraphy had involved sending pulses of radio waves. Radiotelephony required a continuous radio signal, called a carrier wave. Even when there is silence on a radio program, the carrier wave is being transmitted. It is a radio-frequency signal, meaning that its frequency is

anywhere from very low up to 300 billion hertz (cycles per second). The wavelengths of the radio waves vary from enormously long—up to many kilometers—down to 1 mm (1/25 of an inch).

The frequency range of sound waves is far lower—from around 20 hertz to 20 kilohertz (1 kilohertz or kHz is 1,000 hertz). The audio signal from the microphone, representing the sound waves, is combined with the carrier wave. One way of doing this is by modulating, or altering, the amplitude (strength) of the carrier wave so that it varies in exactly the same way as the microphone signal. This is called amplitude modulation (AM) and is used for LF (low-frequency or long-wave: 30–300 kilohertz, 10,000–1,000 meters) and MF (medium-frequency or medium-wave: 300–3,000 kilohertz, 1,000–100 meters) transmissions.

Another method of modulation is used for higher frequencies, which are measured in megahertz (1 megahertz = 1 million hertz). VHF, or very high frequency, is 30–300 megahertz, 1–10 meters; UHF, or ultrahigh frequency, is 10 centimeters–1 meter, 300–3,000 megahertz. Here the method of modulation is frequency modulation

AM AND FM

A low-frequency sound signal can be added to a high-frequency radio carrier wave either as variations in strength (amplitude modulation, AM) or in frequency (frequency modulation, FM).

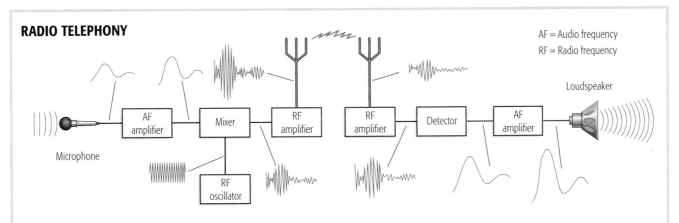

RADIO TELEPHONY

AF = Audio frequency
RF = Radio frequency

Microphone

AF amplifier

Mixer

RF amplifier

RF oscillator

RF amplifier

Detector

AF amplifier

Loudspeaker

The transmitter combines the microphone's audio-frequency signal with the oscillator's radio-frequency signal and transmits the result. The receiver picks up the RF signal, detects (extracts) the AF signal, amplifies it, and sends it to the speaker.

(FM). The amplitude of the carrier stays the same, but its frequency is varied, higher frequency representing higher amplitude of the original audio-frequency signal. Frequency is much less prone to distortion by atmospheric conditions than amplitude is, and as a result FM can give better sound quality.

VHF and UHF signals are short-range because they can penetrate the reflective layers high in the atmosphere, so they are not bent around the Earth as the lower-frequency signals are. VHF transmitters have to send their signals in tight beams along a line of sight to relay masts mounted on high ground. VHF is used by local radio stations, while lower-frequency AM signals are used for making national and international broadcasts. UHF is used for transmissions between the ground and artificial satellites, which orbit the Earth above the reflective layers in the atmosphere.

MOBILE PHONES

Cellular telephones operate with low-power radio in order that users on the same frequency in different parts of the area served do not interfere with one another. It also makes it possible

to have small phones, and there is less worry about potential risks to health with lower-power phones.

The area served is divided into "cells" (hence the name "cellular phone" or "cellphone"), each of which is served by one base station. It receives and transmits calls to and from the phones in its cell and the base stations of neighboring cells. Neighboring cells use different sets of frequencies so that users in the two cells do not interfere with each other. But unadjacent cells can use the same frequencies. The frequencies are in the UHF band. Cells differ in size, but are typically a few kilometers (or a few miles) across.

When a mobile phone user makes a call, the phone first transmits identification numbers to the base station, which keeps track of which phones are in its cell. The phone sends on one frequency and receives on another one, so that the two parties can both send and receive continuously, without having to switch, as with a traditional walkie-talkie or CB radio.

If the user crosses into another cell, the phone detects the weakening of the signal from the base station and requests "reregistration" in another

☞ *See also* Messages through the air **7** : 36; Talking along wires **7** : 34; Pictures through the air **7** : 42

cell. The base station arranges a "handoff" with the base station of the cell where the signal is increasing in strength. The phone switches to a new pair of frequencies provided by the new base station.

A large city may need hundreds of base-station towers. In the United States several competing companies generally use each one.

SATELLITE COMMUNICATION

The enormous increase in radio, TV, phone, and computer data traffic, all demanding radio channels, has led to the use of higher and higher frequencies. These waves penetrate the reflective layers in the Earth's atmosphere, and so they are not bounced around the globe as are LF, MF, and HF (high-frequency, or short-wave) radio transmissions. They have to be relayed around the world by communications satellites, or comsats.

The great majority of comsats share a single orbit 35,800 kilometers (22,240 miles) above the equator. Here they orbit the Earth in 23 hours 56

MOBILE PHONES

The area covered by a mobile-phone system is divided into reception cells, each served by a single base station with a receiving/transmitting antenna. Antennas in neighboring cells operate on different frequencies so that they do not interfere with each other. Sending and receiving frequencies are automatically allocated to a phone when a conversation begins. Signals travel between base stations via central control. The frequencies on which the phone operates are automatically changed if the user takes it from one cell to another.

△ **Telephone on the move**
Mobile phones, or cellphones, have proved astonishingly popular. New-generation phones provide a range of data services, including e-mail and Internet access.

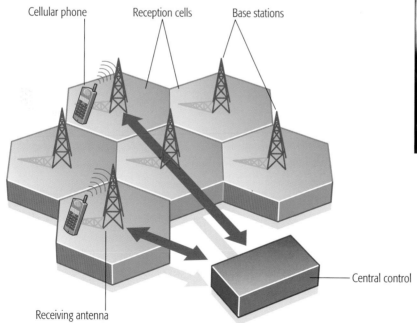

Cellular phone   Reception cells   Base stations

Central control

Receiving antenna

minutes, precisely the time it takes the Earth to rotate once. Hence each satellite in this "geostationary" orbit seems to be permanently fixed in one position in the sky. That makes it easy to keep ground stations locked onto it to send and receive transmissions. A comsat has a dish-shaped receiving antenna to pick up signals from a particular Earth station. It amplifies them and sends them from another dish antenna toward another Earth station. It can also relay signals in the opposite direction between the two Earth stations.

A phone signal passing from the ground via a comsat has to travel at least 71,600 kilometers (44,500 miles), and the reply has to travel an equal distance. This introduces a time delay in conversations of at least half a second, and possibly more. New satellite systems, including the Iridium and Globalstar systems, consist of many satellites in low orbits. Being at low altitude, they can communicate directly with mobile phones, offering a vast range of new services, with no noticeable delay in conversations.

DIGITAL SERVICES

All aspects of telecommunications are being revolutionized as they become *digital*. A digital signal is one that consists of a sequence of digits (numbers).

Digital signals have several great advantages over analog signals. They give high quality. They are easily processed by computers, which work with digits. More of them can be packed into a given bandwidth (spread of frequencies). They are less vulnerable to distortion in transmission, and errors that do occur in them can be detected and corrected.

SATELLITE RELAY

Radio dish antennas on communications satellites (comsats) receive signals from the ground, amplify them, and beam them down to another ground station. The huge solar panels provide electricity for several years. Comsats relay TV, radio, and data signals around the world. They move in 24-hour orbits, 35,800 km (22,240 miles) above the equator, so they seem to remain fixed over one point on the Earth. Each receives signals from a particular ground station and sends them on to another one or to another comsat. Some Russian comsats and some military satellites have used lower orbits.

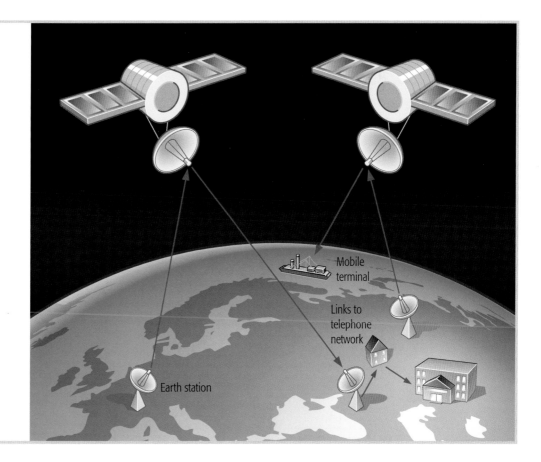

Mobile terminal

Links to telephone network

Earth station

Pictures through the air

After radio, inventors soon found ways of sending pictures over long distances using radio waves. The result—television—has now become global in its scope, with color, stereophonic sound, and teletext. The home TV set will soon be offering access to goods, services, and the Internet, in addition to TV programs.

ELECTRIC CURRENTS SEEM capable of doing anything. If they can convey sounds over immense distances, why not moving pictures seen at the same time that the events are happening? Many inventors struggled to achieve this in the 1920s and 1930s. Common to all the systems was one basic principle: A scene has to be broken down into a pattern of dots of varying brightness, a sequence of electronic signals representing these dots has to be transmitted, and the same pattern has to be reassembled on a screen in the viewer's receiver.

The first scheduled public broadcasts were made by the BBC (British Broadcasting Corporation) in 1929 using a system invented by

▽ **Global TV**
A television camera relays a tennis championship to a global audience. Satellites make it possible to view events anywhere in the world on television.

TELEVISION RECEIVER

A television picture is made up of glowing dots of three colors: red, green, and blue. There is a separate beam of electrons for each color. The screen is coated with either dots or stripes of substances called phosphors, which glow the appropriate color when struck by the electron beam.

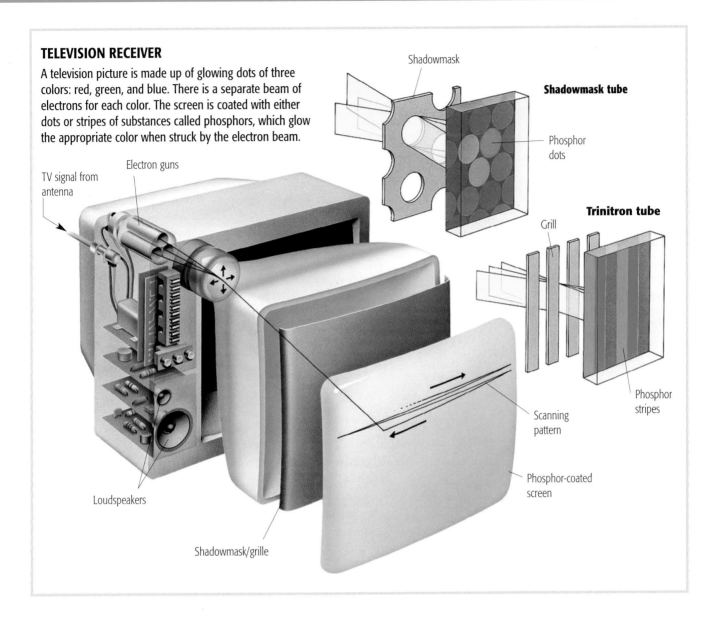

Shadowmask

Shadowmask tube

Phosphor dots

Trinitron tube

Grill

Electron guns

TV signal from antenna

Phosphor stripes

Scanning pattern

Phosphor-coated screen

Loudspeakers

Shadowmask/grille

Scotsman John Logie Baird, which used a rotating mechanical wheel in the camera and the receiver. By 1936 the BBC had abandoned Baird's system, which produced an image consisting of 240 lines, in favor of an all-electronic one with 405 lines. Electronic systems were also used in the first regular U.S. TV transmissions, which were made by NBC from 1939.

The television tube developed from the cathode-ray tube, a glass tube containing a vacuum in which an electrical terminal, the cathode, is heated so that it gives off electrons. The electrons are accelerated by a

potential difference to form a cathode ray, or beam of electrons, that travels to the other end of the tube. The cathode-ray tube was invented as a scientific research tool by the British scientist William Crookes and was developed into a television device by Boris Rozing, a Russian, and his student Vladimir Zworykin, working in the United States.

THE TV CAMERA

In a modern television camera light from the scene is separated into red, blue, and green beams. Combinations of these three primary colors are

43

☞ *See also* Messages through the air **7** : 36; Talking through the air **7** : 38; Uses of vacuum tubes **9** : 12

SCANNING THE PICTURE

A TV picture consists of over a million dots of colored light arranged in 525 lines. Thirty pictures are displayed every second. Each picture is displayed in two stages. In the first stage the odd-numbered lines, 1, 3, 5, ..., are scanned. At the end of the scan the electron beam "flies back" to the beginning and scans the even-numbered lines, 2, 4, 6, ... When the picture is complete the whole sequence begins again. This *interlacing* of odd and even lines reduces flicker in the image.

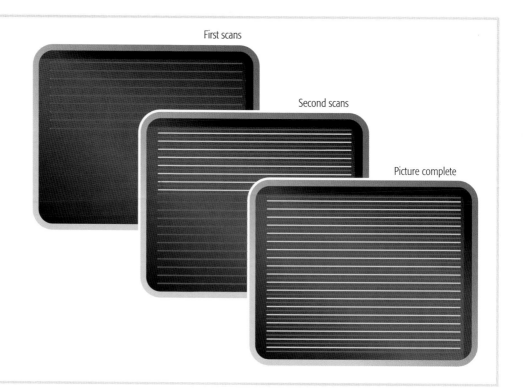

First scans

Second scans

Picture complete

enough to represent any color. Each beam is passed into a separate camera tube, which converts its image into a signal.

The currents from the three tubes are combined to make one signal that modulates a VHF or UHF radio wave. As a result, the signal that is broadcast contains information about the red, green, and blue parts of the scene in front of the camera, as well as an audio signal for the sound.

THE TV RECEIVER

The TV signal is picked up by the viewer's antenna, and the signal is sent into the TV set in the form of a modulated AC electric current. In the receiver electronic circuits separate the signal into its red, green, and blue parts. They are sent to the picture tube, which is a sophisticated cathode-ray tube. Each signal controls a separate electron gun. It is a device in which a hot cathode gives off a cloud of electrons. The electrons are accelerated by electric fields so that a

thin beam of electrons leaves the gun. The three electron beams go through scanning magnets, which are electric coils that bend the paths of the beams electromagnetically. The beams scan the inside of the receiver's screen from side to side and top to bottom.

The inside of the screen is coated with dots or stripes of substances called phosphors. There are three kinds on the screen: one glows red, another blue, another green. A mask ensures that each beam reaches only the phosphor that glows the right color. When the phosphors are arranged in dots, the mask used is a shadow mask, containing accurately positioned holes. In a Trinitron screen, in which the phosphors are arranged in stripes, the mask is a grill of vertical slits. The number of electrons varies from moment to moment, separately in each beam, controlling the brightness of that color in that part of the image.

Where red and blue dots are both equally bright, magenta will be seen;

red and green together make yellow; blue and green make cyan. Red, blue, and green together make shades of white or gray.

Thirty different images are displayed each second (25 in some countries), but each one is scanned twice—once on the odd-numbered lines, once along the even-numbered ones—to reduce flicker. In the United States the image is made up of 525 lines; in most other countries there are 625 lines.

HIGH-DEFINITION TV

HDTV, or high-definition TV, offers a far sharper picture because it has 1,125 or more lines. It also makes a wider screen possible. These techniques call for huge amounts of information to be sent each second over the program channel. They depend crucially on computerized data compression—reducing the amount of data needed to send the information.

With interactive TV viewers can use a hand control to send signals back to the program company while viewing. They can choose different camera viewing positions during a sporting event, send opinions to a discussion program, or order goods and services from a shopping channel.

Compact portable TV sets have been developed in which the screen consists of an array of solid-state devices rather than a vacuum tube. Some use LED (light-emitting diode) displays in which each pixel (picture element) gives out light. Others use liquid-crystal displays in which each picture element allows light to pass in varying amounts according to the brightness of the picture at that point.

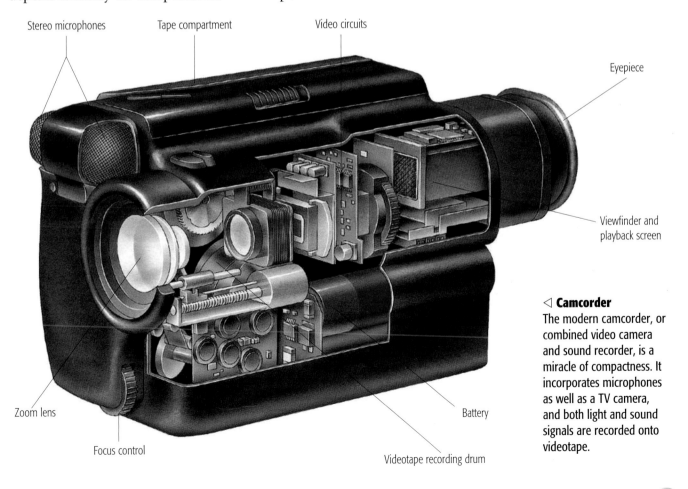

Stereo microphones   Tape compartment   Video circuits

Eyepiece

Viewfinder and playback screen

Zoom lens

Battery

Focus control

Videotape recording drum

◁ **Camcorder**
The modern camcorder, or combined video camera and sound recorder, is a miracle of compactness. It incorporates microphones as well as a TV camera, and both light and sound signals are recorded onto videotape.

❶ Can it conduct?

Some substances allow electric current to flow through them—they are called conductors. Other substances do not allow electric current to flow through them—they are called nonconductors or insulators. In this project you test various substances to find out whether they are conductors or insulators.

In this and other projects in this set it will be very useful to have some lengths of wire with small alligator clips at one end, although you can make do with paper clips and aluminum tape instead. To connect wires to an ordinary flashlight battery, you can use plain tape to connect aluminum tape to the ends (and wind the connecting wires around the aluminum tape). Another way is to put a paper clip at each end of a flashlight battery and hold the clips in place with two rubber bands stretched along the length of the battery. You can then connect wires to the paper clips. Finally, you could use a 6-volt lantern battery or a 9-volt battery because these types have terminals you can wind wire round. However, if the project needs a bulb, make sure it is a 6-volt or 9-volt type if you use one of these higher-voltage batteries. You will be told if you need to use a particular type of battery.

What you will need

- A battery
- Two lengths of wire with alligator clips at one end
- Another length of wire
- A flashlight bulb
- A bulb holder
- Articles to test: paper, coins, eraser, paper clip, rubber band, metal spoon, plastic spoon, safety pin, wooden ruler, steel nail, piece of string, pencil

What to do

Screw the bulb into the bulb holder, and attach the wires to the bulb holder and to the battery as shown in the illustration. Test your collection of articles one

at a time by clipping the alligator clips to them. The article completes a circuit; and if it allows current to flow through the circuit, the bulb will light up—the article is a conductor. If the bulb does not light up, the article is an insulator. As you test them, put each article into one of two groups, one group for all the conductors and the other for all the insulators. Can you see what the substances in the "conductors" group have in common? What about the other group (the insulators)?

The conductors are all metals. This group will contain

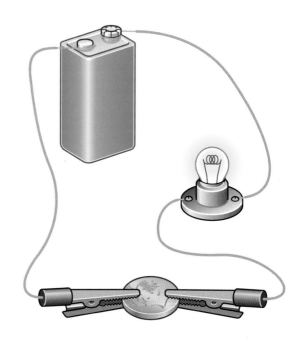

Test each article to see if the bulb lights up.

such items as coins, a paper clip, a metal spoon, a safety pin, and a steel nail. This is a property shared by all metals: they all conduct electricity.

The insulators, on the other hand, are a wide variety of materials, and they are all nonmetals. They include such items as paper, an eraser, a rubber band, a plastic spoon, a wooden ruler, a piece of string, and a pencil. Paper, rubber, plastic, string, and wood are all insulators—plastic is commonly used for the insulation on electrical wiring.

☞ *See pages 6–7 for more about* **conductors** *and* **insulators***.*

❷ Briefly bright

Inside an electric bulb there is a piece of very thin wire called a filament. When electricity flows through the wire, the wire gets very hot and gives off light. A gas that does not support burning (such as argon or nitrogen) fills the bulb and prevents the filament from burning away. In this project you will make an electric bulb. But because your bulb will contain air, it will light for only a very short time indeed.

What you will need

- A battery
- Two lengths of wire with alligator clips at one end
- A small piece of Styrofoam (the base of a Styrofoam cup will do)
- A small glass jar
- Two 7.5-cm (3-in.) steel nails
- A thin strand of steel wool

What to do

Push the nails carefully through the Styrofoam with the heads just sticking up. Tease a strand of fine wire from some steel wool, and wind its ends around the pointed ends of the nails. Place the arrangement inside the glass jar as shown in the illustration. Connect the alligator clips to the heads of the nails. Connect the other end of *one* wire to the battery. Then watch carefully as you touch the end of the other wire onto the other battery terminal.

The thin wire between the nails acts like a filament in an electric lamp. When you passed electric current through it, it rapidly got hot and became red, but soon burned away. But for a brief moment you had an electric bulb. It took two inventors, the American Thomas Edison and an Englishman named Joseph Swan, several years to perfect their first electric bulb, using a carbon fiber as the filament.

☞ *See pages 14–17 for more about* **resistance**.

When you touch the wire onto the battery terminal, the filament will glow red hot.

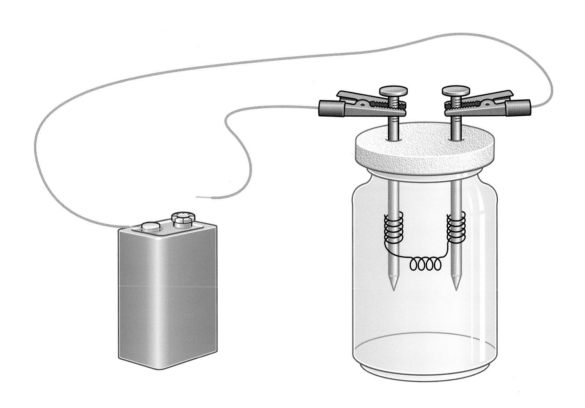

❸ Which switch?

Electricity is a very convenient source of power—just count how many things in your home run on electricity. For all of them, including the lights in each room, you use a switch to turn them on and off. In this project you will make some working switches.

What you will need

- Two small blocks of balsa wood or very dense Styrofoam
- Five 15-cm (6-in.) lengths of wire with the insulation stripped from each end
- A battery
- Five thumbtacks
- Two paper clips
- Two flashlight bulbs
- Two bulb holders

What to do

For the first switch place one thumbtack through the loop at one end of a paper clip and push it into the balsa wood (or Styrofoam) after winding one end of one wire around it. Wind one end of another wire around another thumbtack and push it too into the balsa wood—position it less than a paper clip's length from the first thumbtack. Attach the other end of that wire to the battery. Take the end of the first wire, to the bulb holder, and attach it. Finally, take a third wire, and use it to connect the bulb holder to the battery. The whole setup should look like the illustration.

When you swivel the free end of the paper clip so that it touches the second thumbtack, the circuit is completed, and the bulb lights up. When you swivel it away again, the circuit is broken, and the bulb goes out. The paper clip acts as the moving part of an electric switch.

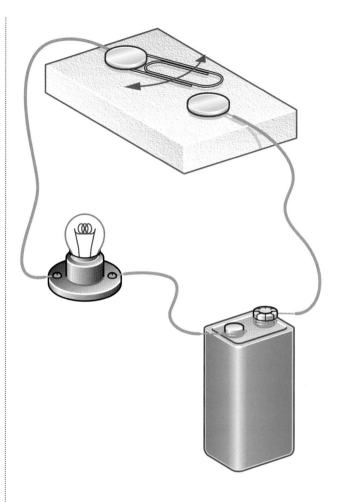

Moving the paper clip from side to side switches the bulb on and off.

Disconnect the wires, bulb holder, and battery. You will now use them to make a two-way switch to control two bulbs. The switch is made in a similar way, but this time the paper clip can swivel between two different thumbtacks. Study the second illustration to see how to do this and how the five lengths of wire need to be connected, with two bulb holders in the circuit. When you swivel the paper clip one way, one bulb lights up. When you swivel it the other way, the other bulb lights up. If you can move the paper clip from side to side fast enough, you can make the bulbs flash on and off in turn.

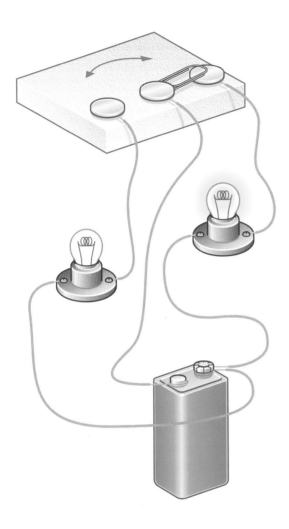

Switch the paper clip back and forth fast enough, and the lights will flash on and off in turn.

☞ See pages 14–17 for more about **circuits** and **switches**.

---

❹ Electric heater

In Project 2 you made a short-lived electric lamp. The filament burned away because it got very hot. In this project you will use a thicker piece of metal as an element to demonstrate the principle of the electric heater.

What you will need

- A 1.5-volt battery (AA type)
- Aluminum foil (kitchen foil)
- Scissors

What to do

Cut a strip of foil about 15 cm by 2.5 cm (6 in. by 1 in.) and fold it in half twice lengthwise. The folded foil is the element of our heater. Curve the element into a shallow U shape, and using one hand, hold it against the ends of the battery and count to 10 slowly. Now feel the element with your other hand. It is getting hot. *Do not leave the element across the battery any longer—it can get very hot indeed.*

Like all metals, aluminum is a good conductor of electricity. But when it is very thin, like the foil in this project, the passage of electric current through it heats it up. You could not make an electric room heater with an aluminum element since it would get too hot and soon burn away. Instead, room heaters have elements made of metal alloys that get only red hot and do not burn up.

☞ See pages 18–19 for more about the **heating effect** of an electric current.

The aluminum foil gets hot, but do not hold it in contact with the battery for too long.

❺ Series or parallel?

When there are several components in an electric circuit, there are two main ways of connecting them. You can put them in a chain, like beads on a necklace, so that the same current flows through them all, one after the other. Components connected like this we say are in series. Alternatively, one wire can connect all the contacts on one side of each component and attach them to one terminal of the battery. Another wire connects the contacts on the other sides of the components to the other terminal of the battery. Components connected like this we say are in parallel.

What you will need

- A battery
- Six 15-cm (6-in.) lengths of wire with the insulation removed from each end
- Three bulb holders
- Three flashlight bulbs

What to do

The easiest way to find out how to wire the three bulb holders is to look at the illustrations. The first arrangement, with the bulb holders in line, is the series circuit. The other is the parallel circuit. Connect the series one first, and remember how the bulbs look. Then connect the holders in parallel. Do the bulbs look any different?

In the series circuit the electric current was reduced because it had to pass through each bulb in turn. As a result, the bulbs were not very bright. In the parallel circuit the full current from the battery went through each bulb, and they were all as bright as if only one was being lit. However, there is a price to pay—the battery would run down three times as fast with the parallel arrangement as it would with the series arrangement.

☞ *See pages 8–11 for more about **series and parallel circuits**.*

Each of the bulbs wired in parallel gets the battery's full voltage—the bulbs are bright.

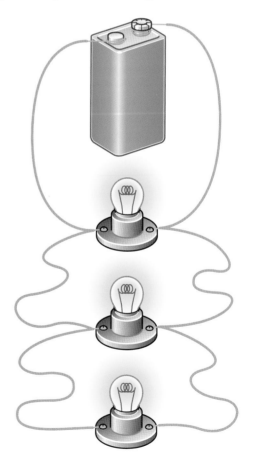

Bulbs wired in series have to share the voltage between them—the bulbs are not bright.

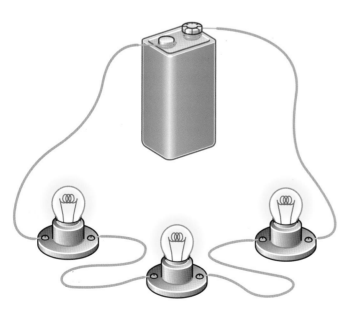

❻ Which wire is best?

Two main things affect how much electric current will flow along a length of wire: how thick it is and how long it is. In this project you will examine these factors and find out which kind of wire is best.

What you will need

- A battery
- Two 15-cm (6-in.) lengths of very *thin* wire (such as the finest type of fuse wire)
- Two 15-cm (6-in.) lengths of very *thick* wire (such as from large straightened-out paper clips)
- Two 15-cm (6-in.) lengths of ordinary bell wire
- Two lengths of bell wire about 2 m (6 ft) long
- Bulb holder
- Flashlight bulb

What to do

The connections are the same for each part of this project—just follow the illustrations. Try out, in turn, thin wires, thick wires, ordinary wires, and long ordinary wires. Each time, look at the brightness of the bulb.

The brighter the bulb, the greater the current flowing along the wire. With very thin wire the bulb is not very bright. With very thick wire the bulb is bright, although the wire is stiff and difficult to handle. The short ordinary wire also produces a bright bulb. But the very long ordinary wire does not pass as much current, and the bulb is not as bright. So it would seem that ordinary wire is best for most purposes, as long as the wires are not too long.

☞ *See pages 14–17 for more about* **resistance**.

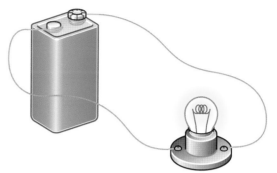

Thin wires produce a dim bulb.

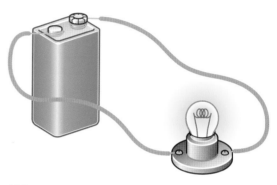

Thick wires produce a bright bulb, but do not bend easily.

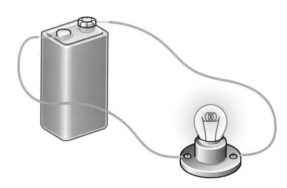

Ordinary wires bend easily and produce a bright bulb.

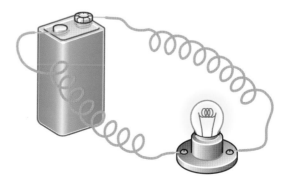

Very long ordinary wires produce a dim bulb.

Glossary

Any of the words printed in SMALL CAPITAL LETTERS can be looked up in this Glossary.

Other terms that are explained in an entry are printed in *italic*.

alternating current (AC) Electric CURRENT that flows first in one direction, then in the other, alternating many times each second. AC is used for domestic electricity supply and many other electrical applications.

alternator A GENERATOR that produces ALTERNATING CURRENT.

ammeter An instrument for measuring electric CURRENT.

ampere (A) The SI unit of electric CURRENT. A current of 1 ampere (often abbreviated to "amp") is equal to a flow of 1 COULOMB per second.

anode A positive electrical terminal on a device such as a BATTERY. ELECTRONS flow into the device through the anode. See also CATHODE.

battery A device that generates electric CURRENT by a chemical reaction. Strictly, a battery consists of several identical units called CELLS, as in a car battery. However, single cells are now invariably called batteries too.

capacitance Also called capacity, the ratio of the stored electric CHARGE on an electrical device or other object to the VOLTAGE applied to it.

capacitor Also called a condenser, a device that stores electric CHARGE.

cathode A negative electrical terminal on a device such as a BATTERY. ELECTRONS flow out of the device through the cathode. See also ANODE.

cathode ray A stream of ELECTRONS produced by the heated CATHODE in a VACUUM TUBE.

cell A device that produces electricity by a chemical reaction. The word has been replaced in ordinary usage by BATTERY.

charge A property of some subatomic particles and some larger objects that makes them exert forces on one another. Charge can be of two kinds, positive or negative.

circuit A network of electrical components that performs some function.

coil In electricity a spiral of wire through which CURRENT flows. The MAGNETIC FIELDS of the current in the different turns of the coil add together to make a large magnetic field; the coil is then an electromagnet.

commutator Part of a GENERATOR or MOTOR that converts ALTERNATING CURRENT or voltage into DIRECT CURRENT or voltage.

condenser See CAPACITOR.

conductance The ability of an electrical component or other object to pass an electric CURRENT. The higher the conductance, the lower the RESISTANCE.

conductor A material or object that allows electric CURRENT to flow through it.

core A piece of iron placed in a COIL to make the coil a more powerful ELECTROMAGNET. When current flows in the coil, generating a MAGNETIC FIELD, the core becomes strongly magnetized.

coulomb (C) The SI unit of electric CHARGE. It is equal to the charge carried by 6.24 billion billion ELECTRONS.

current A flow of electric CHARGE. The current from the domestic electricity supply, from generators, and from batteries consists of a flow of ELECTRONS. Positively charged IONS form part of the current inside some types of battery, moving in the opposite direction from a flow of electrons.

direct current (DC) Electric CURRENT that flows in one direction all the time, though it may vary in strength.

dynamo An electrical GENERATOR, especially one that produces DIRECT CURRENT.

earth See GROUND.

electric field A pattern of electrical influence surrounding an electric CHARGE or created by a varying MAGNETIC FIELD. At each point in space the field has a particular direction and strength.

electric potential At any point the energy derived from ELECTRIC FIELDS that a positive unit CHARGE would gain if brought to that point from infinity. All objects tend to move in such a way as to lose energy, so positive charges tend to move from positions of high potential to positions of lower potential, while negative charges move the other way. Potential is measured in VOLTS. See also POTENTIAL DIFFERENCE.

electromagnet A device that develops a MAGNETIC FIELD when electric CURRENT is passed through it. It consists of a COIL with a CORE.

electromagnetic induction The generation of an ELECTROMOTIVE FORCE by changes in a MAGNETIC FIELD.

electromagnetism The interlinked phenomena of electricity and magnetism. Every electric CURRENT generates a MAGNETIC FIELD. Changes in a magnetic field cause the development of E.M.F. or VOLTAGE and tend to cause current to flow.

electromotive force (e.m.f.) An electrical influence that tends to cause electric CURRENT to flow. Emf is exerted by BATTERIES and electric GENERATORS. It is measured in VOLTS, and is also called POTENTIAL DIFFERENCE or voltage.

electron A subatomic particle, found in every atom, that carries NEGATIVE CHARGE. Most electric CURRENTS consist of electrons in motion.

electrostatic induction The movement of electric charges on an object caused by an ELECTRIC FIELD.

e.m.f. See ELECTROMOTIVE FORCE.

energy The ability of a system to bring about changes in other systems. In electricity the stored chemical energy of a BATTERY can make electric CURRENT flow. An electrical GENERATOR uses the energy of fuel to make electric current flow. Electric current is converted into other forms of energy where required (e.g., light in a light bulb).

farad (F) The SI UNIT of CAPACITANCE. If 1 COULOMB stored on an object raises the object's ELECTRIC POTENTIAL by 1 VOLT, that object has a capacitance of 1 farad. The farad is a very large unit, and the microfarad (1μF, 1 millionth of a farad) and picofarad (1 pF, 1 billionth of a farad) are commonly used.

frequency The rate at which some cyclic process repeats. The frequency of ALTERNATING CURRENT is the number of times per second that the current reaches a maximum in one direction.

fuse A piece of wire that melts (fuses) when the current passing through it becomes too large. This prevents the current from flowing, thus protecting any electrical device connected in SERIES with the fuse.

galvanometer A sensitive device for measuring CURRENT.

generator A machine that produces an electric CURRENT. It contains COILS that are rotated in a MAGNETIC FIELD. This generates an ELECTROMOTIVE FORCE in the coils by INDUCTION.

ground Also called earth, a connection to an electrical CIRCUIT into which CURRENT can flow freely. It is often a metal rod or pipe, such as a water pipe, that literally enters the ground.

hole A position in the crystal lattice of a SEMICONDUCTOR material at which an ELECTRON is lacking. When a neighboring electron jumps into the gap, the hole effectively moves in the opposite direction.

induction See ELECTROSTATIC INDUCTION; ELECTROMAGNETIC INDUCTION.

insulator A material that is a poor conductor of electric CURRENT. Examples are rubber, many plastics, and wood. ("Insulator" is also the name given to a poor conductor of heat.) See also CONDUCTOR.

ion An atom or molecule that has lost or gained one or more ELECTRONS so that it has an electrical CHARGE.

joule (J) The SI unit of ENERGY. One joule is the energy needed to move a charge of one COULOMB through a POTENTIAL DIFFERENCE of one VOLT.

magnetic field The pattern of magnetic influence around an object.

metal Any of a group of chemical elements in which electrons can flow easily, making them very good CONDUCTORS.

motor A machine that converts ENERGY, usually electrical energy, into motion.

ohm (Ω) The SI unit of RESISTANCE.

ohmmeter An instrument for measuring RESISTANCE.

Ohm's law At constant temperature the CURRENT through an electrical component or circuit is approximately proportional to the ELECTROMOTIVE FORCE across it. This relation (it is not really a "law") is enormously important despite being true only for some materials.

parallel Two electrical components in a circuit are connected in parallel if the current divides to pass through them separately. See also SERIES.

photoelectric effect The ejection of ELECTRONS from a solid (especially a metal) when light falls on it.

potential difference Also called voltage, the difference in ELECTRIC POTENTIAL between two points. It is measured in VOLTS. The higher the potential difference, the greater the force tending to move charges between the points.

power The rate of expending ENERGY. The power of a MOTOR is the rate at which it expends energy in producing motion. The power of a GENERATOR is the rate at which it produces electrical energy.

resistance A measure of how a material or a component resists the passage of electric CURRENT through it. The higher the resistance, the less current will pass when a given POTENTIAL DIFFERENCE is applied across it.

resistor An electrical component with a known RESISTANCE, used to regulate CURRENT and VOLTAGE in a circuit.

semiconductor A material that has a RESISTANCE intermediate between that of an INSULATOR and a CONDUCTOR. In *n-type semiconductors* current is carried by negatively charged ELECTRONS. In *p-type semiconductors* current is carried by HOLES.

series Two electrical components in a circuit are connected in series if the same current passes through both of them in turn. See also PARALLEL.

static electricity An electric CHARGE on an object that has lost or gained ELECTRONS.

superconductivity The property of conducting electricity with no RESISTANCE at all. Some METALS do this when cooled close to absolute zero (–273.15°C/–459.67°F). New complex substances have been developed that superconduct at higher temperatures (though not yet as high as 0°C).

transformer A device that increases or decreases the VOLTAGE of ALTERNATING CURRENT.

vacuum A completely empty space in which there are no atoms or molecules of any substance.

vacuum tube An airtight glass tube in which electricity is conducted by ELECTRONS passing through a partial VACUUM from a CATHODE to an ANODE.

volt (V) The SI unit of POTENTIAL DIFFERENCE.

voltage See POTENTIAL DIFFERENCE.

voltmeter A device for measuring POTENTIAL DIFFERENCE.

watt (W) The SI UNIT of POWER, equal to a rate of expending ENERGY of 1 JOULE per second.

Set Index

Page numbers in *italics* refer to illustrations. Volume numbers are in **bold**. Main entries are in **bold**, with the relevant page numbers underlined. Page numbers in parentheses ( ) indicate that a subject is covered in the activities at the end of the volume. For example:

Electromagnet

    making 8: *17,* 24-27, (50) shows that all references are in volume 8, that there is a relevant illustration on page 17, and the main entry is on pages 24 to 27. A project on page 50 is about making electromagnets.

A

Abbe, Ernst **4:** 33
ABS **9:** 34
absolute zero **3:** 11, 45
absorbers, heat 3: 38–41
AC *see* alternating current
acceleration 2: 18–21
  circular motion **2:** 22
  constant speed **2:** 22
  and force 2: 18–21
  inclined plane **2:** *11*
  Newton's laws **2:** 19
  vector **2:** 21
accelerator
  linear **10:** 25–26
  particle **10:** 24, 25
  underground **10:** *27*
accumulator **6:** 42, 44–45
acetylene **1:** 10
acids **6:** 39, **9:** 25, 26
acoustics **5:** 35
action and reaction **2:** 19–20
  balloon rocket **2:** (49)
additive process **4:** 26
Advanced Gas-cooled Reactor **10:** 32
advertising signs **6:** *30,* 32
air 1: 8
  compressed **1:** 32, *34,* 35
  convection currents **3:** 30–31, 50
  drafts **6:** 23–24
  expansion **3:** (46–47)
  flow **1:** 40, (51)
  ionization **6:** 23, *24,* **10:** *23*
  lifting **1:** (50)
  liquefying **1:** 29
  liquid **3:** 45
  molecules **6:** 23, *24*
  pressure 1: 32–35, (46–47)
  thermal conductivity **3:** 29
  vibrating columns 5: 16–19, (47)
  weight **1:** 8
air bags **1:** (50)
air resistance *see* drag
air-conditioning **3:** 43, **6:** 27
airfoil **1:** 40, *41*
airplanes **1:** 39, 40–41
  fly by wire **9:** *43,* 44–45
  navigation **2:** 17
airship **1:** *8,* 10, 21
air-traffic controllers **2:** 16
alcohol **3:** 11, *19*
alcohol thermometer **3:** 13

ALEPH detector **10:** *26*
alloys **1:** 45
alpha particles **9:** 7, **10:** 15, 16, *17,* 21
alternating current (AC) 7: 20–21
  advantages **7:** 20
  DC conversion **9:** 10, *13, 33,* (49)
  frequency **7:** 23
  generation **7:** 25, 27
  reversal **8:** 35, 40
  voltage change **7:** 20–21
alternating current motor *see* electric motor, AC
altimeters **1:** 9
aluminum **1:** 19, 45
  anodized **6:** 40
  expansion **3:** 25
  extraction **6:** 41
  ions **6:** 34
  semiconductor impurity **9:** 18, *19,* (51)
  thermal conductivity **3:** 28
aluminum foil **7:** (49)
  mirror from **4:** (47)
alveolar sounds **5:** 41
ammeter **7:** 11, 12, *13*
Ampère, André **8:** 32
ampere (A) **2:** 7, **7:** 11
amplification
  FET **9:** 23
  high-power **9:** 13
  junction transistor **9:** 22
  paper **5:** (51)
  radio **9:** (47)
  semiconductor **9:** 19, 33
  vacuum tube **9:** 10–11
amplitude **5:** 10, *11*
amplitude modulation (AM) **7:** 38
analog signals **7:** 41
anastigmatic lens **4:** 35
aneroid barometer **1:** 9–10
angle of dip **8:** *13*
angle of incidence **4:** 14, 18
angle of reflection **4:** 14
angle of refraction **4:** 18
  critical angle **4:** 21
animals
  infrasound **5:** 28, 29
  navigation **8:** 14, *15*
anion **6:** 34
anode **6:** 31, 32, 33, 38, **9:** *10*
anodizing **6:** 40
ant **9:** *24*
antinode

flute **5:** *19*
  pipe **5:** *17,* 18–19
  string **5:** *13*
  woodwinds **5:** *18*
antiparticle **9:** 15, **10:** 17, 18
Apollo mission **1:** 35, **5:** *32*
apparent depth **4:** (48–49)
Apple II **9:** 36
aqueduct **1:** *42,* 43
Arab clothing **3:** *40*
Arab traders **8:** *6*
arc light **4:** 7
arch **1:** 43–44
archaeology, dating **10:** 21
archer **2:** *28*
Archimedes **1:** 20, **2:** 36
Archimedes' principle **1:** 20, (47)
area
  resistance **7:** 15, (51)
  thermal conduction **3:** 28
arm
  as lever **2:** 37
  robotic **9:** *32,* 33
arsenic **9:** 18, *19,* (50)
astigmatism **4:** 35
Aston, Francis **10:** 10, 11
astronomical telescope **4:** 38–39
atmosphere **1:** 36
  pollution **6:** 26
  pressure **1:** 8, 9
atmospheric engines **1:** 33
atom 1: 6–7, **10:** 7
  charge **6:** 6, 34–35, **7:** 6, **10:** 6–7
  chemical reactions **10:** 9
  cooling **1:** 28
  crystals **1:** 15
  electrons **1:** 6, 7, **6:** 6–7, 11, **10:** (47)
  hydrogen **6:** 34
  images **9:** *6*
  ions **6:** 34–35
  isotopes **10:** 9–11, (47–48)
  magnetism **8:** 7
  models **10:** 7, (46)
  nucleus **6:** 6, 11
  particle accelerator **6:** *21*
  relative atomic mass **10:** *10,* 11
  scale **9:** (46–47)
  solids **1:** 14, 26
  stability **9:** 17
  structure **9:** 6–7, **10:** 6–7, (46)
  theories of structure **9:** 9
  versatility **10:** 38–39
  vibration **3:** 6, 7, 27
atom bomb **10:** 28, 29, 31
atom smashers 6: 21, **8:** 21, **10:** 24–27
atomic clock **2:** 8
atomic number **10:** 9
atomic pile **10:** 30
atomic time **2:** 8
atomic weight *see* relative atomic mass
atto- (prefix) **2:** 9
attraction
  electric currents **8:** 22, 23
  ions **6:** 34

static electricity 6: 8–11, (46–47), (48–49)
  see also magnetism
audibility **5:** 36–37, *37*
audible sound range **5:** 26
audiotape **8:** 16, 19
auditory canal **5:** 38, *39*
aurora **8:** *12*
autoclave **1:** 24
automobile *see* car
autopilot **9:** 44

B

bacteria **2:** *6*
bagpipes **5:** *18*
Baird, John Logie **7:** 43
balance **3:** *38,* 39
  equilibrium **2:** 33–34
  forks **2:** (46)
  seesaw **2:** 34, (47)
  tightrope **2:** *35*
balances **2:** 8, 12–13
balloon **1:** 10, 18, 21, **3:** *22,* 23
  rocket **2:** (49)
  sound conduction **5:** (46)
  static electricity **6:** (48–49)
barcode **9:** *44*
Bardeen, John **9:** 18
barium **10:** 28
barometer **1:** 8, 9–10
base units, SI system **2:** 7, 9
bassoon **5:** 19
bats, ultrasound **5:** 26–27
battery 6: 38, 42–45, **7:** 9, *10*
  automobiles **6:** *42,* 44–45
  Daniell cell **6:** 44
  DC current **7:** *21*
  dry **6:** 44
  fuel cell **6:** 45
  Leclanché cell **6:** 44
  mercury oxide **6:** 44
  mine tunnel **7:** 10
  nickel-cadmium **6:** 44
  NIFE **6:** 45
  parallel **7:** *11*
  polarization **6:** 43–44
  primary **6:** 42, 44
  secondary **6:** 42
  series **7:** *11*
  wet **6:** 44
battleship **3:** *20*
bearings, magnetic **8:** 43
beats **4:** 43
Becquerel, A. E. **10:** 16
bel **5:** 32
Bell, Alexander Graham **7:** 34
bell, electric **8:** 28–29
bells **5:** *22,* 23
  glass **5:** (49)
  spoon **5:** (50–51)
belt drive **2:** 43–44
bent straw illusion **4:** *19*
Bernoulli's equation **1:** 39, 40
beryllium **10:** 24, (46)
beta particles **10:** 15–16, *17,* 21
bevel gears **2:** 45

bias
  diodes **9:** 21–22
  FET **9:** 23
  microchip manufacture **9:** 26
  semiconductors **9:** 23
bicycle *see* cycle
Big Bang **10:** *7*
bimetallic strip **3:** 13–14, 24
binary code **9:** 28
binocular microscope **4:** 40
binoculars **4:** 38
biological computers **9:** 45
biological shield **10:** 36, 38–39
biologists **10:** 22–23
bioluminescence **4:** 7
birds, thermal lift **3:** 30, *32*
bits **8:** 18, **9:** 28, 30
black body **3:** 39
black clothing **3:** *40*
black smokers **3:** (49)
blast wave **5:** 8
blasting **2:** 30–31
block and tackle **2:** 43, *44*
body, activity measurement **8:** 20
body imaging **8:** 19–20
body temperature **3:** 13
Bohr, Niels **9:** 9, **10:** 7
boiling 1: 22–25, **3:** 18, *19*
boiling-water reactors **10:** 36
bolts **2:** 41
bombs **8:** 23
bonding
  covalent **1:** 7, 15
  intermolecular **1:** 15
  ionic **1:** 7, 15, **6:** 34, 36
  metallic **1:** 15
  solids **1:** 15
boron **9:** 27, **10:** 24, (46)
bottle opener **2:** *39*
Bourdon gauge **1:** *9*
bow **5:** 12
bow and arrow **2:** *28*
Boyle, Robert **1:** 11
Boyle's law **1:** 11
braking **1:** 37, **8:** 43, **9:** 34
brass instruments **5:** 19
Brattain, Walter **9:** 18
breaking point **1:** 44
breeder reactors **10:** 32–33, 40
brick, thermal conductivity **3:** *28*
bridge **1:** *42,* 43–44, 45
  expansion **3:** *24,* 25
  Tacoma Narrows **5:** 30
broadcasting
  radio 7: 38–41
  TV 7: 42–45
brush, electric motor **8:** 35, *36*
bubble chamber **10:** 18
bubbles **1:** 13, 23
bulbs, Christmas tree **7:** *14*
bulbs, incandescent *see* electric light
bulldozers **1:** 36
bullets **1:** 38–39, **2:** 30
Bunsen burner **1:** 40

Further Reading

General Reference

Albert Einstein and the Frontiers of Physics (Oxford Portraits in Science) by Jeremy Bernstein. Oxford University Press Children's Books

Basic Physics: A Self-Teaching Guide by Karl F. Kuhn. John Wiley & Sons

Essential Physics by Philippa Wingate. E D C Publications

Eyewitness Visual Dictionaries: Physics by Jack Challoner. DK Publishing

Great Scientific Discoveries (Chambers Compact Reference Series). Chambers

How Things Work: The Physics of Everyday Life by Louis A. Bloomfield. John Wiley & Sons

Illustrated Dictionary of Physics. E D C/Usborne

Introduction to Physics by Amanda Kent *et al.* E D C Publications

Janice Vancleave's Physics for Every Kid: 101 Easy Experiments in Motion, Heat, Light, Machines, and Sound (Science for Every Kid) by Janice Pratt VanCleave. John Wiley & Sons

Physics in the 20th Century by Curt Suplee *et al.* Harry N. Abrams

Physics Lab in the Home (Physical Science Labs) by Bob Fredhoffer. Franklin Watts

Physics Made Simple by Ira M. Freeman, William J. Durden (Designer). Doubleday Books

Physics Principles and Problems by Paul W. Zitzewitz. MacMillan Publishing Company

Physics: The Easy Way by Robert L. Lehrman. Barrons Educational Series

Science and Technology by Lisa Watts. E D C/Usborne

Science School by Mick Manning, Brita Granstrom (Illustrator). Kingfisher Books

The Flying Circus of Physics by Jearl Walker. John Wiley & Sons

The Kingfisher Science Encyclopedia, Editor Charles Taylor. Kingfisher Books

This Strange Quantum World & You by Patricia Topp. Blue Dolphin Publications

Turning the World Inside Out and 174 Other Simple Physics Demonstrations by Robert Ehrlich, Jearl Walker. Princeton University Press

Websites

The Children's Science Center – http://www.cyberstreet.com/csc/

How Stuff Works – http://www.howstuffworks.com

Science Laboratory – http://www.cbc4kids.ca/

The Why Files – http://whyfiles.news.wisc.edu/index.html

Electric Current

Circuits, Shocks and Lightning: The Science of Electricity (Science at Work (Austin, Tex.)) by Celeste A. Peters. Raintree/Steck-Vaughn

Electricity and Magnetism (Fact Finders Series) by Mike Clemmet. Parkwest

Electricity and Magnetism (Making Science Work) by Terry Jennings *et al.* Raintree/Steck-Vaughn

Electricity and Magnetism (Yesterday's Science, Today's Technology) by Robert Gardner, Doris Ettlinger (Illustrator). Twenty First Century

Electricity (Make it Work! Science) by Alexandra Parsons. Two-Can Publishing

Electricity (Straightforward Science) by Peter D. Riley. Franklin Watts

Electronic Communication (Hello Out There) by Chris Oxlade. Franklin Watts

Science Explorer: Electricity and Magnetism by Prentice Hall School Group. Prentice Hall

Photographic Acknowledgments

Abbreviation SPL Science Photo Library

6 Chris Knapton/SPL; **8** Martin Bond/SPL; **10** Georgina Bowater/The Stock Market; **14** Corbis/Steve Chenn; **19t** Charles D. Winters/SPL; **19b** Andrew Syred/SPL; **20 & 22** U.S. Department of Energy/SPL; **24** Martin Bond/SPL; **28** Mark Bolster/International Stock/Robert Harding Picture Library; **32** SPL; **34** Dr. Jeremy Burgess/SPL; **36** John Mead/SPL; **40** Robert Harding Picture Library; **42** Philippe Plailly/SPL. All artwork copyright © Andromeda Oxford Ltd